INSTANT Parties

Luann Grosscup &
Jo O'Connor Tazelaar

Meadowbrook Press
Distributed by Simon & Schuster
New York

Library of Congress Cataloging-in-Publication Data

Grosscup, Luann.
   Instant parties / by Luann Grosscup and Jo O'Connor Tazelaar.
     p. cm.
   ISBN 0-88166-393-X (Meadowbrook)
   ISBN 0-743-21616-4 (Simon & Schuster)
    1. Entertaining. I. Tazelaar, Jo O'Connor. II. Title.

TX731 .G76 2001
642'.4—dc21　　　　　　　　　　　　　　　　　　00-069194

Managing Editor: Christine Zuchora-Walske
Editor: Angela Wiechmann
Proofreader: Megan McGinnis
Production Manager: Paul Woods
Desktop Publishing: Danielle White
Cover Art: Doug Oudekerk
Illustrations: John Clarke

© 2001 by Luann Grosscup and Jo O'Connor Tazelaar

All rights reserved. No part of this book may be reproduced or transmitted in any form or by any means, electronic or mechanical, including photocopying, recording, or using any information storage and retrieval system, without written permission from the publisher, except in the case of brief quotations embodied in critical articles and reviews.

Published by Meadowbrook Press, 5451 Smetana Drive, Minnetonka, Minnesota 55343

www.meadowbrookpress.com

BOOK TRADE DISTRIBUTION by Simon & Schuster, a division of Simon and Schuster, Inc., 1230 Avenue of the Americas, New York, New York 10020

05 04 03 02 01　　　10 9 8 7 6 5 4 3 2 1

Printed in the United States of America

Dedications

For my second-grade teacher, Mrs. Virginia Doersch.
With the irresistible enticements of triple-ruled manila paper
and fat green pencils, she sparked my love affair
with the written word. —L. G.

For my children, Alison and Sean, and for
my husband, Jim, whose amazing support
is eclipsed only by his smile. —J. O. T.

Acknowledgments

To Tim, Meghan, and Andrew Grosscup, my gratitude
for your love, patience, and support. —L. G.

To my siblings, Tom, Kathleen, Brian, Paul, and Shawn, without whom neither life nor I would be nearly as funny, thank you. And for your sense of irony and general irreverence, I salute you. —J. O. T.

We'd also like to express appreciation to our friends for their inspiration, ideas, feedback, and blatant enthusiasm for our parties. Thank you Andy Hanahan, Lane and Cindy Pierce, David Weiss, Barb Kessner, Jim and Jane VandeVelde, Gloria Dunne, Jim Williams, and Doris Herndon.

A very special thank-you to our agent, Mary Breslin.

Contents

Introduction vii

FANTASY

Fright Fest 2
Strangers* 6
It's a Marvelous Night for a Moondance 10
Frank Sinatra's Real Swingin' Affair* 13
Summer of Love 17
Noel Coward's Brief Encounter* 22
Havana! 27
Magical Mystery Party 31
Bond. James Bond.* 35
Marrakesh Express* 40
¿Señora, Que Quiere? 44

PARTIES THAT GET YA MOVING

Outdoor Summer Games for Big Kids 52
Hide-and-Seek in the Dark and on the Floor 57
Pool (Swimming)* 60
Pool (Pocket) 64
Hans Brinker, or The Silver Skates 68
We're Rollin'! 73
Any Given Sunday 77

DINING—FINE OR OTHERWISE

Commune Dinner 82
Done Yer Duty 86
Blue Plate Special 90
Shangri-La-De-Da (de da) 94
Bakery Dinner 99
Ragin' Cajun* 103

*Denotes an elegant, *swell-egant* affair.

v

Cookbook Pass-Around 107
Divide and Conquer* 111
Chinatown 115

ODD BUT AMUSING

Wild Abandon 120
Progressive Leaf Raking 124
Hubristic Tour 127
Munich Meets Milwaukee 131
Whine and Cheese 136
Story Weaver 140
Pajama Game 144
Venus Flytrap 148
Showtime! 153
Hot Wax Night 157
New Blood 161
Radio Days* 165
Okay, but Not at My House! 169
Happy Trails to You! 173
Vice-Free Party 176
Virtual Party 180
Come As You Are! 183
Hootenanny 188

MUSINGS

The Antidote 192
Sunday Morning 196
Fireside Chats 199
The Equinox, the Solstice, and the Sky 202
Beethoven, Books, and Bull* 206

Afterthoughts 210
Index 211

*Denotes an elegant, *swell-egant* affair.

INTRODUCTION

We've all invited people over for next Saturday night only to kick ourselves when next Saturday afternoon rolls around. With guests descending in T-minus-4 and counting, we wonder: *Whatever* could have possessed us to invite ten people for dinner? We wish there were some way to give a party exactly when the mood strikes us...

Say hello to the instant party!

You can prepare for any of the fifty parties in this book in less than a day. Some are even doable in less than an hour! Hosting an instant party virtually assures you'll give a party only when you're in the mood. Another great reason for the short-notice route is that the weather will always cooperate, and your parade will never again be rained upon.

Each instant party includes suggestions for standard party basics: invitation, menu, props and décor, entertainment, and music. Each party also has a theme. Why a theme, you ask? Well, let's put it this way: How many times can you "just have people over"? Themes give your parties purpose and direction. After all, why not try something different? You've already done everything you've tried before! And heck, you're just having a party. The survival of humankind is not at stake.

It's not necessary to be an aristocrat or a magician to host an instant party. We assume you either own or have access to most of the basics. If you have tableware, a music collection, a wee bit of know-how when it comes to preparing a menu, and a few this-and-thats, we're not kidding when we say you can whip up any of these parties in a matter of hours. We'll show you how to pull it together in such a timely manner, you won't even break a sweat. How much time you'll need will depend on how elaborate you choose to be with the planning—for example, whether you'll order from a restaurant or do the cooking yourself.

To get an idea of how much prep time you'll need for the parties, check out the key at the beginning of each chapter. Here's how it works:

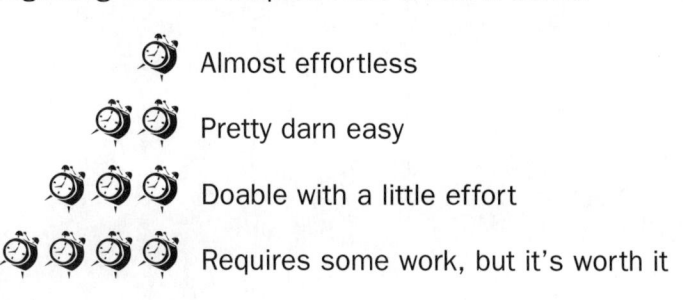

⏰ Almost effortless

⏰⏰ Pretty darn easy

⏰⏰⏰ Doable with a little effort

⏰⏰⏰⏰ Requires some work, but it's worth it

If there's one caveat when it comes to instant entertaining, let it be this: Under no circumstances do we want to hear one word of apology escape your lips because "it's something you just threw together at the last minute." Do you think for a moment those fascinating bohemian poets in Paris apologized over and over because their places looked, well, the way they looked when those hordes of unexpected guests dropped in? Don't make noises that suggest "this isn't going to be anything special." (With that approach, your guests may choose to stay at home until you give a party that *is* something special!)

Make no mistake: We still host long-planned, big-deal, over-the-top, blow-out parties, and we're sure you do, too. But we find ourselves holding fast to the belief that instant is the way to go if we want to "do this more often." And we don't know about you, but we happen to think that whenever inspiration and opportunity happen simultaneously, well, that's special.

Instant parties are the wave of the future. They're happenin'. They're *now*. Literally. It's what *instant* means. So how lucky are you to have found this book?

Lean in a little closer, friend, 'cause it only gets better from here.

Fantasy

Fright Fest

One spring break we decided to pack up the kids and head for the historic river town of Sainte Genevieve, Missouri. Sainte Genevieve promised to be warmer than Chicago in April, and perhaps there would be the added surprise of blossoms already in bloom. When we arrived, we got an added surprise, all right. But instead of the fragrance of blossoms, we got ghosts!

We checked into a little cottage in the heart of the small town. "Oh, it's just darling," we gushed. "All lovely and quaint." Then one of the kids, reading what previous guests had written in the guest book, piped up, "Mom, this place is haunted." Our cottage, it seemed, was home to the ghost of a riverboat gambler who liked to play cards in the second-floor bedroom, roll dice, and scare the living bejeepers out of guests.

We got everyone settled into bed that night and ever so casually left all the lights on. We tried buttering up the ghost by telling him good-night, saying what a lovely place he had, and so on. It didn't work. No sooner did our heads touch the pillows than we heard invisible dice rolling on the polished hardwood floor. Ghostly laughter followed us as we flew down the stairs, pillows in hand, shrieking, "He's up there!"

We were actually delighted when one of the kids got the flu the next day, forcing us to leave immediately. Unnerving as the haunting was, however, we admitted that we loved that delicious feeling of being totally creeped out. So we came up with a party that allows us to be completely in control of how scared we're willing to get.

INVITATION

By Phone

The only sound your prospective guest will hear is your slow, scary breathing—so slow and so scary that it sounds as if it's coming directly from the grave.

Then before he can hang up, you'll say, "Scared ya, didn't I?" Give him a moment to say "yes, you did" or "no, you didn't," then add, "Come on over tonight at seven for a picnic and more of the same. Bring your spooky stories and your flashlight."

By E-Mail

"Many ghosts and forms of fright have started from their graves tonight."
—Longfellow

Join us tonight at 7:00 for a picnic and an evening of horror! Bring a tale from the crypt and a flashlight. Call before 5:00.

"Do not fail us, lest *you* be next!"
—[your last name]

MENU

There's something wonderfully incongruous about a wholesome picnic and fearsome, frightful tales from the beyond. When we hosted this party, we called it our "Urban Legend Picnic." We spread tablecloths and blankets on the floor, or you can do so out on the grass, if weather permits. Since it's a picnic, use plastic or paper tableware to make clean-up easy.

Food

Could anything be simpler?

- Chicken: Pick some up at one of the thousands of places where chicken is available. Serve it hot or cold.
- Biscuits: You can usually get them from where you get the chicken.
- Baked beans: They can be from the deli or from the jar. Serve in coffee mugs.
- Cole slaw
- Brownies

Beverages

Anything in bottles is just fine with us.
- Beer
- Wine coolers
- Soda

PROPS AND DÉCOR

- Set out tablecloths, blankets, cushions. We want you on the floor or the ground, but if you need to, go ahead and use the table—just don't tell us.
- Place flashlights in odd areas to create truly creepy lighting. Have extra batteries on hand. Sure as Shinola, people will bring flashlights, but they'll try to turn them on and the batteries will not work. We practically guarantee it.
- "BELIEVE IN BLOODY MARY!" scrawled in red lipstick on the bathroom mirror will get you some mileage. When we hosted this party, we wrote those words backward on a sheet of paper and taped it to the wall above the shower curtain. It was only visible when the guest was looking in the mirror.

MUSIC

We know you're tempted to use one of those "scary sounds" Halloween tapes or CDs, but we advise against it. They're distracting. Don't use any music that will encourage people to sing along either. Here's what we found worked rather well:

- Slow Native American music
- Aboriginal music
- Classical, especially anything including a harpsichord
- Gregorian chants
- Anything in a minor key
- Anything by Philip Glass
- Anything by Ravi Shankar

ENTERTAINMENT

- Make sure it's dark before the creepy stuff gets going. Since you asked your guests to each bring a frightful tale, hopefully they have done just that. Inform them ahead of time that their tales may be "urban legends" (found on the Internet or in books dedicated to the subject), tales of horror from any source, incidents that actually happened, or their own creations. Following dinner, each guest will be allowed a slot of time to tell his or her story. (In case that long-winded guest goes on and on for more than ten minutes, ask in a stage whisper, "Can I get anyone anything?" It will pull the guest out of his storytelling trance and get him to wrap it up. But that's about all you can do, since you're the one who asked for the story.) When all the stories are finished, the guests will vote on whether each story was fiction or fact.

- How about a game of something we used to play as kids called "Feeeeel This Man's Booooones"? One person goes into another room. The rest of the group prepares things for the person to touch. (You'll need to have these things ready in advance.) All the lights are extinguished, and someone leads the "victim" into the darkened room where the man's booooones (and other body parts) are kept. Using a shaky voice straight from the crypt, someone presents a body part to the victim and tells him or her to "feeeeel this man's booooones, feeeeel this man's eyebaaaaalls, feeeeel this man's entraaaaails, feeeeel this man's liverrrrr." Here's how it works:
  - Use real meat bones for the bones, such as rib bones or chicken bones. Or use a Milkbone dog biscuit.
  - Eyeballs can be made from peeled grapes.
  - Cooked spaghetti in a plastic zipper bag makes wonderful innards.
  - Slightly warm milk makes nice blood.
  - Okay, *fine*, a bratwurst would be just perfect for that.
  - Do you have any skin left from that chicken? It would work for this man's skin, too.
- Any chance you have a neighbor who's unable to attend but wouldn't mind creeping out your guests a time or two? How about asking the junior-high kid next door who'd love to do something like this? If you're all outside, have him run through the house, waving flashlights. Or if you're all inside, a little window-screen scratching might just give everyone the heebie-jeebies, too.

So you tell us, regarding our "Ghost in Sainte Genevieve" story: Did we make it up? *Or did it really happen?*

Strangers

We find this party intriguing—oh yes, we surely do. Both having been married a long time, we thought it would be positively tantalizing to go to a party where everyone comes with a completely different persona. Wouldn't our husbands be...mysterious? We imagined ourselves off in a corner with those strapping hunks of love that we married, flirting madly, finding each other terribly amusing, and being swept off our feet all over again. My, what things we'd have to talk about if we pretended we weren't married!

People are invited to come to this party with completely new personas. Your guests may *look* like the same old crowd, but tonight, they're not. No one knows anyone else. You'll all meet for the first time. Always looking to stir the pot, we encourage couples not to arrive together but to "meet" each other at the party (wink wink, nudge nudge). As host, you'll choose the locale and era of your party: Paris in the twenties, Istanbul in the sixties, perhaps. Or your place, right here, right now.

There are no rules here. Guests can keep the same personas all night or change them at whim. For example, if the twine salesman from North Dakota isn't getting much mileage, perhaps the Navy SEAL will. We suggest you have dossiers available for those who don't come with personas. If a few dullards slip through the door thinking they're just going to be themselves, your response is no, they're not. You'll have several characters waiting in the wings from which they can choose: a British consul, exotic dancer, staid and dour man of the cloth, explorer, smuggler, spy. Same goes for those who picked annoying or obnoxious personas. Just hand them the dossiers along with a simple "Here, pick one, because you're not going to keep on being the one you came in as."

Enjoy this party. It's a chance for adults to do what we all did so well in kindergarten—playing "Let's Pretend."

INVITATION

By Phone

"Yvonne, we'd like you to engage your imagination in an evening of fanciful intrigue! Come over at seven. Bring your alter egos and whatever props you'll need to make them come alive." Then explain the concept. If Yvonne has any imagination at all, she should be able to pull together an idea or two in short order.

By E-Mail

Come and engage your imagination! Choose whoever you wish to be this evening at 7:00. Play one role or play many as you and other guests discover one another for the first time.

RSVP to Stephen Ascot III (a.k.a. Bob) by 5:00.

MENU

Use your pretty china and linen, and lay out the food in a buffet. That way, your guests can just saunter over (in character, of course) and help themselves.

Food

This party features cocktail nibblies. If you choose an exotic locale and want the food to fall in line, you may want to take the path of least resistance and give your offerings oh-so-clever names rather than serve authentic dishes. Mata Hari Meatballs? Shrimp à la Marie Laveaux? Here are a few ideas to get you going:

- Jalapeño poppers
- Chicken wings
- Hot cheese-and-chili dip with tostada rounds
- Fresh shrimp with cocktail sauce
- Nuts
- Spinach dip served in a bread round
- Cocktail meatballs
- Cheese and crackers
- Fruit

Beverages

The bar's wide open tonight. You'll have all the typical cocktail party offerings. We encourage you to have everything available to allow guests to serve themselves.

- Beer
- Wine
- Scotch and soda
- Gin and tonic
- Rum and Coke
- Blender drinks: Margaritas are usually a crowd pleaser. Have the recipes and ingredients available and then turn the guests loose with your blender. (We'd hate for you to man the blender all night and then get that look of disdain that bartenders get when asked to make yet another blender drink.)

PROPS AND DÉCOR

- At the very least, do something to make your house look different. When we hosted this party, we took everything out of the dining room, brought in easy chairs, and called it the Speakeasy Lounge. No, *really,* people were impressed!
- Here's another idea that goes along with mystery, intrigue, and changing identities. How about changing the lighting every hour? Have your bulbs and candles ready in advance, and it won't take more than a moment to create great effects.
  - When guests arrive, go with soft pink or low-watt incandescent bulbs.
  - After an hour or so, set your room aglow in candlelight.
  - Another hour into the party, go with blue bulbs. You'll get that feeling of a vintage nightclub.
  - Use the candles again as you allow the bulbs to cool.
  - Finally, switch to black bulbs. Don't we all feel just a little naughty in a black-lit room? It's so underground. Safety first, though: Black bulbs can get incredibly hot.

MUSIC

We want you to change music when you change the lighting. Have these selections set up in advance, and give yourself about an hour's worth of each genre. Go with what your guests like, but make it diverse.

- Nostalgic: Tony Bennett, Glenn Miller
- Motown: Smokey Robinson, Marvin Gaye, The Temptations, The Four Tops
- British Invasion: The Beatles, The Dave Clark Five, Petula Clark
- Jazz: Basia, Harry Connick, Jr., George Benson, Grover Washington, Swing Out Sister, The Manhattan Transfer
- Sexy Latin: Casolando, Buena Vista Social Club, Antonio Carlos Jobim
- Calypso, island-y stuff: Jimmy Buffett, Harry Belafonte

ENTERTAINMENT

Each guest's persona will be pretty darn entertaining, and meeting "new" people throughout the evening should keep everyone amused. But you'll also need a few well-timed bursts of "herding the herd" to give a bit of cohesiveness to the party:

- Charades: Every half-hour, choose someone to act out a charade. Write a famous name on each of several slips of paper. Place the slips in a box, and have a person pick one. The performer gets three minutes to act out the name of the famous person. Don't make the names too obscure, or people will start crabbing at you, "Well, who's ever heard of Blah-Blah-Blah, anyway?"
- Mission Possible: As the guests arrive, give them each a slip of paper with an activity to perform in whatever character they happen to be at the time indicated. Here are some examples:
  - "At 10:00, go up to your neighbor's husband and suggest he do the only honorable thing: Step aside so you and Marge can be truly happy."
  - "At 10:35, start a fight by saying to one of the female guests, 'I absolutely did *not* say your bosom looks like ten pounds of goods in a five pound sack! I merely said that support is *always* important!'"
  - "At 11:30, take a swig of your drink and declare loudly, 'What kind of rotgut *is* this?'"
- Musical chairs: Call it something else, like "Strangers in the Night," if it'll make you feel more dignified. This is a chance for some wayward fanny to end up on some unsuspecting lap.

> We hosted this party to stellar reviews, and we're here to tell you that once you get everything set up, the party practically runs itself. So latch on to the rare opportunity to stop being the host, and slip into someone more comfortable.

It's a Marvelous Night for a Moondance

How many times have we caught ourselves smiling indulgently while watching some PBS special about isolated Amazon tribes who won't allow their photos to be taken for fear of losing a portion of their souls?

Instead of dismissing their beliefs as primitive quirks, we should throw off the trappings of our own ethnocentricity and listen to what they're saying. At least they have the good sense to realize when their souls are being chipped away! Contrast their beliefs to those who spend hour after tedious hour sitting in traffic on the expressway while on the way to the battlefields of the boardroom. In time, they feel the insidious chiseling away of their souls yet never have a clue as to the cause.

On a warm night last October, the moon rose full and red. Somehow, a dickens must have gotten into us, because before long, our behavior mirrored that of the primitive Amazon tribe to the point where we felt we could be the subjects of a PBS special ourselves. The full moon prompted us to round up a group of friends, drive to an open field, and spend an hour dancing under the sky. We weren't wearing loincloths or anything, but we were following our instincts, trying to hold on to the few pieces of our souls that had worked their way loose.

You know what? It did the trick. After an hour or so, we returned to home base feeling reconnected to nature, passion, and meaning.

Don't ask us to explain how this works. We don't know. But we do know this: If everyone on the expressway spent equal time dancing under the moon, the world would be a better place.

INVITATION

By Phone

"Jean, we're going moondancing! I'm gonna pull into your driveway in about ten minutes and honk the horn. Come running!"

By E-Mail

"It's a marvelous night for a moondance!"

I'm picking you up at 7:00 tonight, and we'll dance under October skies! Be ready!

Call me before 5:00.

MENU

The spirit of the moondance may not move you until you get a load of the moonrise that night. Fortunately, you can pull this party off in a matter of minutes. Toss the hooch and chow into a picnic basket. Include napkins, a corkscrew, wineglasses, paper plates, several sharp knives, a small cutting board, and a tablecloth or blanket.

Food

A quick pit stop at the grocery store is all that's required if you don't have the following items on hand:

- Loaves of crusty French bread
- Wedges of smoked Gouda or other favorite cheese
- Juicy fruit of all colors and shapes

Beverages

- Hearty red wine (Bordeaux, Burgundy, cabernet sauvignon)
- Light, fruity white wine (Chardonnay, Waipara sauvignon blanc)
- Sparkling white wine (asti spumante)

PROPS AND DÉCOR

Even *we* could not begin to improve upon the backdrop of a full moon, star-peppered sky, and night filled with fireflies.

MUSIC

Bring a boom box or use your car's sound system. Choose music that transports you to a place in time when life was utterly carefree. The music we chose for our night of moondancing was *The Best of 3 Dog Night*. We drove to a remote location far enough from the nearest neighbor so we could crank it up good and loud.

ENTERTAINMENT

You should have seen us! We danced, we spun, we whirled, we cartwheeled. We were truly succulent, wild women and men. We howled at the moon, we broke bread, we drank wine, communing not only with one another but with the universe. We had shanghaied one of our guests from her home, but when we dropped her off a mere ninety minutes later, she was practically weeping, so happy for the opportunity to reclaim the bits and pieces of herself that had fallen by the wayside. We're not going to go on and on, trying to convince you of the magical properties a moondance has to offer.

Once you experience it, however, we bet you'll find yourself checking those little moon pictures on the calendar, following the phases of *la luna*. Sure as we're sittin' here, you'll throw this party again and again.

> The moon is responsible for governing the tide patterns, and for that, it gets all kinds of accolades. But that same gravitational pull gets blamed for making people nuts (ergo, the word *lunatic*) by wreaking havoc with something-or-other in their brains. It's said that the moon's effect on the human psyche is unpredictable. During the night of our moondance, the effect we derived was all organic and primal. And the impact lingered—our moods were really good for a long time.

Frank Sinatra's Real Swingin' Affair

This party screams "Pal Joey." It's all about the era of Frank Sinatra, Dean Martin, Sammy Davis, Jr., and the world they created. In this world, eveningwear was accessorized with a martini glass and a Lucky Strike. This party is all about the smell of smoke in the air and smoldering cigarettes resting on thick ashtrays. It's about smooth Scotch, highballs, and Rob Roys sipped from old-fashioned glasses. It's about pools of electric light from a rash of twenty-watt bulbs softly lighting the room. It's about words like *verve* and *hubbub.*

This is the party our prying eyes observed through the stairway spindles in 1962. We could hear the clinking of ice cubes in glasses and the one shrill female laugh that periodically overrode the muffled banter. There was the *click-click-click* of high heels in rhythm with song lyrics that you could actually understand. All the big people we'd seen working in their yards on Saturdays had now become Frankish and very cosmopolitan.

Are you with us so far? This was a time when men were men, dames wore skirts, and calling someone "sister" didn't necessarily mean she was wearing a habit. Frank Sinatra's Swingin' Affair hearkens back to when America still had one foot in the fifties and when beef and tobacco were good for you. Then and even today, people long for the nightlife of Mr. Francis Albert Sinatra. Have yourself a real swingin' good time.

INVITATION

By Phone

"Laura, did you know we're friends with Frank Sinatra? Well, Frank is hosting a real swingin' affair tonight at our house, and he asked me to make sure you and Joe could be here at seven."

By E-Mail

Frank Sinatra invites you to attend a real swingin' affair tonight at the home of his friends, Sheila and Lee.

Dinner at 7:00. Dancing at 8:00. Proper attire required.

RSVP by 5:00.

MENU

This is the kind of evening Frank would have had when he stopped at Toots Shor's for some good chow between sets. Use a white linen tablecloth, linen napkins, and your good tableware. Serve guests as though at a restaurant. Dim the lights and use candles unless you happen to have one of those small, battery-operated dinner lamps, which would be perfect. Following dinner, clear the table and place everything out of the way in a large plastic storage tub (with a lid). You can completely clean up in less than ten minutes this way.

Food

Frank didn't worry about fat—*you* don't worry about fat. Here's what Frank would have ordered, and we think it's something you can pull together quickly.

- Tossed salad: If you have time, add a few radish rosettes. Use Thousand Island dressing, of course.
- Steaks (broiled medium well): Offer A.1. Steak Sauce or Worcestershire sauce.
- Baked (or nuked) potatoes with butter and sour cream
- Vegetable side dish: Get a frozen selection you can prepare quickly.
- Parker House dinner rolls and butter
- Chocolate cake

Beverages

- With dinner, Frank would have had a mixed drink. But it's your house. Wine? Beer? Ice water?
- Serve coffee and cream with the cake.
- As you clear the table, send your guests to the self-service bar complete with liquor, glassware, ice bucket, swizzle sticks, cocktail toothpicks, lemon curls,

and bowls of olives and pearl onions. As far as drinks go, save the blender for Jimmy Buffett. If Frank couldn't swizzle it, guzzle it, or pour it over ice, he wasn't thirsty. Here are some Frank-approved ideas:

- Beer: No tricks here. Beer was a man's drink, and back then, men didn't like tricks—unless she was wearin' a skoit. (Sorry, couldn't resist.)
- Martinis
- Highballs
- Manhattans
- Rob Roys (Don't you just love that name?)
- Gibsons
- Bull Shots: Combine liquid beef bouillon, vodka, lemon juice, and a bit of Worcestershire sauce and Tabasco. Serve over ice.

PROPS AND DÉCOR

- This party might have taken place in someone's home in the early sixties, and we think you can achieve that effect with a few well-placed props:
    - Lamps: No overhead lighting—lamps only. Use twenty-watt bulbs.
    - Big, heavy ashtrays: It's up to you whether you want people to actually use these in your house, but they make great props. (If you don't want guests to smoke inside, be prepared to smile, hand them one of those heavy pups, and point the way to the "smoking section" on the verandah.)
    - Matchbooks: When we hosted this party, a friend had just returned from Vegas with a cache of matchbooks, and we felt we had hit the jackpot.
    - Small bowls of Spanish peanuts
    - Plain white paper cocktail napkins wherever you have food set out
- Strategically place decks of cards, dice, pads of paper, and nice pens around the room. Notes written on the pads, like "Frank—Dino called" or "Sammy to stop over at 9:00," will add to the ambiance. People actually *do* read these and twitter over them.
- Encourage your guests to dress for the occasion. For the hostess, we'd like an elegant but sleeveless sheath that's cut just above the knee. (If it's January, turn up the heat, but you are going sleeveless!) For him, we'd love

to see a white dinner jacket, but we realize that's not likely to happen. A suit will do nicely, provided he has a Frank-thin tie to go with it. (Watch the tie, though: Too skinny and now it's *West Side Story*-thin.)

MUSIC

The music will be by the Chairman himself, natch. We realize it will be tempting to go overboard, but please, not all Frank, all the time. You should also include music by other artists of the era (the early sixties). Perhaps add a bit of bossa nova to the mix? Keep the following artists in mind:

- Sarah Vaughan
- Stan Getz
- Oscar Peterson
- Dean Martin
- Sammy Davis, Jr.
- Ray Conniff
- Steve & Eydie

ENTERTAINMENT

Think of this as your basic mom-and-dad cocktail party. (Just imagine your mom is Natalie Wood. And Dad? Well, he's Dean Martin.) It's a tried and true combination of good food, cocktails, and fabulous music. But if you want to throw in a few extras, here's what we suggest:

- Frank Sinatra Trivia: If you have time, go to the library and pull out some questions and answers from one of the many books on Frank. Divide guests into two teams and test their Ol' Blue Eyes knowledge. Keep the music going, but turn it down.
- Charades: Write Frank-related movies or songs on slips of paper ahead of time and put them into a natty hat. Use the same teams from the trivia game.

> This party's going to go late. In fact, it may go so late that you'll be wondering how to say goodnight. We've found that the simple offer of "Would anyone like coffee?" usually works like a charm. Some will accept, others will decline, but you'll see a few glances at wristwatches. Offering coffee, it seems, has a way of gently reminding your guests that it's late and you ain't gettin' any younguh.

Summer of Love

We loathe that lame, old cliché that goes "If you remember the sixties, you weren't there." Well, guess what? We remember the sixties and, yes, we were there.

This may shock some younger or more sensitive readers, but here's what we remember about the Summer of Love, 1967: It wasn't so much about *love* as it was about *S-E-X*. But settle down right now, you, because that is *not* where we're headed with this party!

The summer of 1967 was a turning point, a funky juncture where innocence converged with disillusionment. Music got a little edgier. It was not as sticky-sweet as the music from the early sixties but not as raw as what would be released a few years later. The music of 1967 beautifully captured the spirit of the Summer of Love. And that's what this party is all about.

But before we get to the party, here's something else we remember about the sixties—something some of you would love to forget. Remember how much fun you had skinny-dipping in the reflecting pool in Washington, D.C.? And we can only assume your birthday suit dance-and-chant at the Golden Gate Bridge was a scream-and-a-half. But tell us, honestly, did any of you expect the Associated Press to snap your posterior for all posterity? Because here we are, thirty-some years after the fact, and we're curious: Is it a scream-and-a-half when your own college-age kids find those photos of Mom and Dad in *Life,* displaying it all to the world? Just wondering.

INVITATION

By Phone

"Hey, peace, brother! You wanna groove with us tonight about seven? Far out! Just don't wear any of those Establishment threads, okay, man? Be easy, so we can love."

By E-Mail

There's something happenin' here,
People singin' and drinkin' a beer!

It's the Summer of Love, man, and it's happening in my back yard at 7:00 tonight! Call Moonglow Meadow (a.k.a. Dorothy Johnson) before 5:00!

Outtasight!

MENU

This kind of menu might have been served at the free café on Haight-Ashbury: strictly vegetarian, positively organic, and preferably from India. (Or not.) But we did come up with a few ideas we think are pretty authentic, easy, and yummy. Set up a buffet and let guests help themselves. Have blankets and pillows strewn close by so your guests can lie back and chill while they partake of your offerings and each other's conversation.

Food

- Cold rice salad: Cook the rice with chicken, beef, or vegetable stock. When it's cold, add bits of avocado, chives, and toasted sesame seeds. Dress with a mustard vinaigrette dressing and fresh basil leaves. Serve with soy and teriyaki sauce and Mongolian Fire Oil.
- Falafel with cucumber and yogurt sauce
- Pita bread: Brush it with olive oil and sprinkle with Italian seasonings. Soften it under the broiler a few minutes before serving.
- Raw veggies with salad dressing dip
- Pretzel logs with mustard
- Variety of cheeses
- Nuts
- Brownies: Offer them two or three in a plastic baggie (à la bake sale), in a basket, or on a tray. (If any of you young whippersnappers don't understand the significance, ask your mother.)
- Screaming Yellow Zonkers

Beverages

- Beer in bottles or from a keg
- Annie Green Springs, Ripple, Boone's Farm wines: Maybe just a bottle or two of each, for old time's sake. Then feel free to break into your regular stash.
- Colorful Jell-O shooters
- Boilermakers: Remember the garbage-can concoction to which everyone added his or her contribution? You can still do this and make it taste good. Think of the recipe ahead of time, so you can tell each guest in advance what to bring. We're thinking of a Planter's Punch or a variation on that theme. Your guests will wax nostalgic as they dump their ingredients into a (brand-new) small plastic garbage can.

PROPS AND DÉCOR

- Remember to tell your guests to dress the part. You'll want to re-create the ambiance as much as you can, and, of course, everyone will look completely ridiculous in the fashions of 1967. (Personally, we don't think the women's stuff is all that bad, but the men's fashions are beyond description.)
- You'll get the most bang for your buck if you have this party outdoors on a great summer night. But if you want to do it indoors, we won't stop you. If you do hold it outdoors, be sure to create a groovy setting with the following props:
  - Paper Japanese lanterns
  - Colored Christmas tree lights: Even the small lights will work, but if you can get some of those big, honkin' bulbs, all the better.
  - Peace signs
  - Real flowers (preferably daisies) in a glass, Mason jar, or wine bottle
  - Strobe and black lights (Find inexpensive ones at electronics stores.)
  - Unisex "restroom": Hang a white sheet and place a black light behind it. On the sheet, fasten a unisex restroom sign—you know, with the stick man and stick woman. On the reverse side of the sheet (if anyone actually falls for your shenanigan), hang another sign that reads "Just kidding, man! Go in the house!"

- Distribute a Haight-Ashbury type of newsletter, except name it after your street intersection, like the Adams-Harvard Weekly Flyer. Create your own bits of news, using your friends' names. Here are some examples:
    - "Next Tuesday, Lucy and Beanie will show their watercolors on the beach."
    - "Remember to keep saving those box tops for the new free clinic!"
    - "The bake sale was a big success! We collected $42 for Tim and Amy to get their car out of the pound!"
    - "We're saying goodbye to Pigpen, everybody. The shirts got him, and he's heading for Silicon Valley to work for the Man."
    - "Our best to Melissa and Tony—there'll be one more child to carry on in this world! Melissa's got a bun in the oven—three months along!"

MUSIC

The music will make this party, so go the extra mile and get some really great sounds, not to mention a great sound system. Here are some artists who were popular during the late sixties:

- Janis Joplin, solo or with Big Brother and the Holding Company
- The Rolling Stones
- Jimi Hendrix
- The Doors
- Sly and the Family Stone
- The Young Rascals
- Canned Heat
- The Beatles
- Otis Redding
- The Mamas and the Papas
- The Grass Roots
- Buffalo Springfield
- Scott McKenzie
- The Grateful Dead
- Jefferson Airplane
- The Byrds
- Strawberry Alarm Clock

And if you want to be really authentic, get *Billboard Top Rock 'n' Roll Hits: 1967*, featuring the following songs:

- "Windy" by The Association
- "Respect" by Aretha Franklin
- "Happy Together" by The Turtles
- "I Think We're Alone Now" by Tommy James and the Shondells

- And the number one song of 1967 *(drum roll)*: "Little Bit O' Soul" by The Music Explosion (We hear they never had another hit.)

ENTERTAINMENT

- The Maharishi Mahesh Yogi was big during this time, and so were games of trust and togetherness. Here are a few games that will keep the vibes mellow:
  - Spiral circle song game: Everyone lies in a circle with heads touching, feet pointing out. The first person starts a song, ending midphrase. The next person starts a new song that begins with the last word of the previous song. To anyone viewing this scene from overhead, it looks like a Gestalt group gone goofy.
  - Trust circle: Form two circles—ladies on the inside, gents on the outside. Play music as the participants join hands and circle in opposite directions. When the music stops, so do both circles. When the gents are certain there is someone behind each woman, each woman falls backward into the arms of whichever man happens to be behind her. The woman simply has to trust that someone is there to catch her. And you have to trust *us*—it's fun.
- Fill kiddie wading pools with water and set out some garden hoses in case people want to get crazy and wet.
- Get body paint and cheap artist's brushes (or if you'll be painting big beer bellies, house-painting brushes!). Place globs of paint on paper plates, and let guests paint one another. You may wish to have some sixties memorabilia, like Peter Max art, lying around for inspiration.
- For the few, the brave: a plastic drop cloth, Mazola oil, and pure whimsy. Let your guests know ahead of time that they'll need to bring a change of clothes or an old bathing suit if they want to participate in the Mazola Roll. Otherwise they'll be driving home naked. And try explaining *that* to the nice officer.

> We should probably issue a word of warning about this party—especially the Mazola Roll: Let's just say that if the husband was frisky when the evening began, that Mazola Roll isn't going to make him any less so. To review what we told you at the beginning of this chapter, more than being about *love,* the Summer of Love was about *what?*

Noel Coward's Brief Encounter

When my dear friends told me of their plans to lay out, for all, a collection of their best instant parties, I knew at once how I could best lend my support. As these same charming friends, the authors of this book, have been lovely guests at many of the social affairs to which I have played host, it seemed only natural to lend my name to this gathering of elegance and aplomb.

Although I have up to this point been known as a playwright and author, creating this extraordinarily pleasing lawn party was a delight. Indeed, it happens to be named after one of my own best works, *Brief Encounter.* The play, set in 1940s England, was later made into a movie and was nominated for an Academy Award in 1947.

For this party, as with any social gathering, the host is charged with setting the tone for his guests. This, of course, is done by example. There is deportment prescribed for this type of affair, which I can only assume is universally accepted. However, for the less traveled, let us review:

- Should a guest choose to mix perfectly good Scotch with, say, 7 UP, one says nothing.
- Should a guest choose to all but drown the unsuspecting arugula with salad dressing, one says nothing.
- Should a guest choose to extend an invitation for one into an invitation for two, thereby sending the host running willy-nilly for another chair (resulting in the *first* Mrs. Edinfurth being seated elbow-to-elbow with the *second* Mrs. Edinfurth), again, one says nothing.
- However, should a guest endeavor to retrieve caviar with what is clearly a fish fork, well, *this* is too much. Pour yourself some of the aforementioned Scotch and look away.

That much said, shall we carry on then?

INVITATION

By Phone

Naturally, you won't want to appear overly eager. May I suggest you approach your guests with a simple "Nigel, Noel here. We'll be entertaining on the east lawn today. About five, then?"

By E-Mail

My dear friends have also asked that I pen a simple written invitation to comply with their format. Perhaps a little ditty such as this would work?

Though parties of fashion of late
Are curiously now out of date,
While keeping "chin up"
We say "bottoms up!"
To what lies beyond my garden gate.

Kindly telephone me promptly—N.

MENU

While one could present this affair as a dinner party, it would also work well as a brunch or a luncheon. Have your guests join you in a spirited presentation of carrying out the food in wicker baskets or picnic hampers. Set up several tables for your buffet as well as for guests, and cover them with linen. (Nothing too wobbly here, or it's farewell to the pâté.) Carry out your dining chairs or use an assortment of outdoor lawn furniture. For an extra touch of elegance, you may wish to add a pretty pillow for back support on each chair seat. Your dinnerware should be your fine china or earthenware. And do feel free to mix and match, for heaven's sake. Lovely glassware, silverware, and linen napkins complete the look of luxury.

Food

You can create this elegant lawn party with finesse and ease. I'm told that most, if not all, of these items are available through your grocer or at a fine delicatessen, so you will likely be doing very little of the cooking yourself. As for the rest, simply follow the suggestions listed, and you'll enjoy the satisfaction of hosting a fabulous party with very little fuss.

- Hors d'oeuvres tray: Include Mediterranean olives, prosciutto, melon, and assorted crudités. You know, *that* sort of thing.
- Wedge of smoked Gouda
- Crusty French bread
- Various pâtés
- Seedless green grapes as well as strawberries (Always a delight.)
- Boneless pork tenderloin: Marinate, roast, and chill ahead of time, then slice into ½-inch medallions. Each guest should receive four or five of these little lovelies, which is the equivalent of roughly ½ pound of meat per guest.
- Marinated and steamed asparagus tips
- Cold potato salad: Certainly, purchase this from the delicatessen, but add some chopped fresh chives to dress it up a bit.
- Parboiled and chilled baby carrots with grated ginger and lime juice
- Sorbet, cheesecake, light cookies: All enchanting desserts.

Beverages

Set up a bar in your picnic area. Include glassware, corkscrews, bottle openers, and a generous supply of towels, in case of an unfortunate spill. (You do need to address the reality of disposing one's trash, so have a wastebasket nearby.) And I'm sure you know that form over function is never in good taste, so never mind that you don't have silver ice buckets. Chin up, old chap. A supply of galvanized tubs and buckets will work nicely to keep your beverages icy. "Lawn drinks" are all about refreshment, don't you think? Here are some delightful examples:

- Cold, fine beer
- Wine or champagne
- Grasshoppers
- Vodka or gin and tonics with lime
- Ice water, sparkling water, or iced tea served with citrus wedges
- Flavored iced coffees: Flavorings can be purchased from your favorite liquor store, I'm told. And adding Bailey's Irish Cream to coffee is always enjoyable.

PROPS AND DÉCOR

- Kindly note that this is not your everyday event. You may wish to gently remind your guests that the era is the 1940s and the locale is a lovely English lawn, so would they kindly dress accordingly?
- First and foremost, you simply must create a setting for your guests. Whenever you bring the indoors outdoors, it tends to feel elegant, don't you think? In order to do that, you will hold your event in an area somehow cordoned off from the rest of your lawn. You can accomplish this effect in a few simple ways:
  - Lay area rugs on the lawn.
  - Surround your party area with luscious greenery. Intersperse your potted plants with tiki torches. Or you can hang lovely battery-operated paper Japanese lanterns in the trees. (I'm told you can find these at import stores.)
  - Screen off your area with cabana panels. They are simple, versatile, and so lovely, you'll be reticent to take them down. String some line about seven feet off the ground. Use clothespins to hang several lengths of sheer cheesecloth or gauze that reach nearly to the ground. I'm told such fabric is quite inexpensive indeed. Hang white icicle lights behind the panels to create a soft backlight. A caveat about the gauze and the tiki torches: I assume you know to be safety-minded here, old chap. You simply must not allow the gauze and torches to come in contact, you know.
- On the tables, place votive candles in Mason jars filled with sand. A bit of a plebeian look, to be sure, but charming nonetheless. Simple cuttings from your trees or bushes look lovely in jars as well. You may also choose to float flower blossoms in a bowl filled with water.

MUSIC

You likely already know that this era offered fabulous music selections from both sides of the Atlantic. Of course, you'll have a sound system positioned so that the music needn't be played too loud. You'll want it to enhance the mood, not detract from it. However you choose to address your sound system issues, I have included a list of musical artists that I have enjoyed immensely:

- Buddy Rich
- Duke Ellington
- Glenn Miller
- Ella Fitzgerald
- Bing Crosby
- Marlene Dietrich
- Josephine Baker
- Benny Goodman
- Harry James
- Fred Astaire

ENTERTAINMENT

Since this is a party featuring fine dining and music, it is not entirely necessary for you to provide any organized entertainment. However, if you wish, you may suggest charades (known in its time as "The Game.") At Blue Harbour—my charming estate in Jamaica—I have certainly delighted in playing this with the likes of Larry Olivier, Johnny Gielgud, Ian Fleming, and, of course, Tallulah Bankhead. Can you imagine?

Authors' Note: Okay, okay. We all know that Noel Coward did not write this chapter. Actually, Noel Coward hasn't written anything in nearly three decades. He's been dead since 1973.

As daylight becomes dusk, light the candles, breathe deeply, and welcome the fireflies! If the crickets are chirping and the moon is full, you have all the ingredients to create what your guests will no doubt recall as a "place in time." *Truly* delightful.

Havana!

In the fifties, America and Cuba were undeniably involved in a love affair. It was a perfect match. Cubans became enamored with American culture while Americans fell in love with exotic Havana.

Havana touched a place in every being—it made *la vida* just feel good. During the day, warm sun caressed travelers' backs. The air was always heavy with something—be it the salt of the sea, the sweetness of flora, or the succulence of food.

As the sun set upon Havana, tourists dreamed of the evening that lay ahead. The syncopation of the island fell in step with the tourists' own cadence as tan bodies slipped into linen. Havana simmered with expectation. By twilight, Havana moved to a tempo that the tourists could not only feel but also hear, see, smell, and taste.

Fifties Cuba is what you'll offer your guests when you host our Havana! party, a night that captures all the romance and elegance of well-heeled Americans traveling abroad.

Ah, *la vida!* Ah, Havana! Let us begin the beguine!

INVITATION

By Phone

"Hi, Mary. Jim and I will be taking the seven o'clock Caribbean Clipper to Havana this evening. Shall we arrange for your ticket?"

By E-Mail

Can you join us tonight for an evening under the Cuban moon?

Dinner and dancing at 7:00. Let us begin the beguine!

Telefono by 5:00.

MENU

Serve this meal buffet-style and use your best tableware.

Food

While many places in the United States don't have Cuban restaurants or delis, Cuban food is made with ingredients that are readily available. Using these ingredients, you can easily create a taste of the island. Your bill of fare should feature garlic, onion, cumin, lime, and peppers. Here's a sample menu:

- Faux paella: Real paella takes all day to make, and if you're inclined to go the distance, have at it. But you can also put one together relatively quickly by using clam juice and fish or chicken stock instead of water and by coloring the rice bright yellow with turmeric. To the prepared rice, add sautéed scallops, mussels, oysters, chicken, sausage, green peppers, red peppers, yellow peppers, onions, garlic, chopped green olives, and olive oil. (You're going for a "confetti" look.) Bake in an earthenware pan until hot.
- *Picadillo:* This is a ground-beef mixture served on yellow rice with black beans. Prepare the ground beef with bay leaf, garlic, peppers, and onion. Add tomato sauce. It will have a chili-like consistency, but cook until it's thicker. Add water-soaked raisins and one or two finely chopped eggs.
- Ham
- Black beans and yellow rice with sausage
- Cuban bread: Buy a long loaf of soft white bread. French or Italian will do if you can't find authentic Cuban bread. Split and butter the loaf and warm it in the oven under a heavy pan to give it that smashed look.
- Salad: The traditional Cuban salad is simple: lettuce, tomato, and onion served with oil and vinegar.
- Flan: Buy an instant flan right off your grocer's shelf.
- Guava paste: This may be difficult to find unless your area has grocery stores that specialize in Latin cuisine. It comes in a brick, and it's a sweet, thick jelly that comes in different flavors and is enjoyed with fruit and cheese.

Beverages

- Rum highballs: Remember, this is fifties Havana. We won't slap your nose with a newspaper if you make tropical drinks, but Ricky Ricardo would more likely have had a rum and soda with a lime wedge. Or take a cue from the Andrews Sisters and serve rum and Coca-Cola. Adding a wedge of lime makes it a Cuba Libre. Serve in tumblers and keep that ice bucket handy.
- Martinis: That old standby from the fifties crosses all borders and languages.
- Here are a couple of drinks from a recipe book we like, *Memories of a Cuban Kitchen* by Mary Urrutia Randelman and Joan Schwartz (Hungry Minds, 1996). *Ay, madre!* to both of these tasty treats!
  - Havana Yacht Club Cocktail: Combine 2 ounces dark rum, 1 ounce sweet vermouth, dash apricot brandy, and ½ cup crushed ice. Shake in a cocktail shaker. Pour into a chilled cocktail glass.
  - Havana Cooler: Crush mint leaves. In a tall glass, combine 2 ounces dark rum and ice. Fill with ginger ale.
- Daiquiris: Invented in Cuba, so the story goes.
- *Café con leche:* This is strong Cuban coffee made with half coffee, half whole milk, and sugar to taste.

PROPS AND DÉCOR

- Place dim "up lights" in your houseplants. You can accomplish this effect by tucking a small flashlight into the greenery or by placing a small lamp with a low-watt bulb behind a plant. If you don't have plants, we're sure you can illuminate something in your house this way. We'd just like you to enjoy some gauzy and misty lighting.
- Dress up! We don't have too many parties in this book where we ask gentlemen to put on suits and ties, but we think this party warrants it. For the ladies, nice dresses, stockings, heels. If guests feel compelled to add a bit more nostalgia to their looks, that's always fun. The hairdos, the skinny ties, the seams in the stockings. Think color! Think *Coo-bah!*
- This party should be inspired by a night when it's so warm, you want to be on the back patio or indoors with all the windows thrown open. Or when there's four feet of snow, and you wish things could be different.

MUSIC

- Besides the food, the music shares top billing for this party. Crank it up a little louder than you may otherwise be inclined. Here are some artists you may want to feature:
  - Afro Cuban All Stars
  - Barbarito Torres
  - Buena Vista Social Club with Ibrahim Ferrer
  - Casolando
  - Pedro Vargas
  - Tito Puente
  - Herbie Mann
  - Xavier Cugat
  - Stan Getz

- Also keep in mind that there's been a huge growth in contemporary Latin music, such as Ricky Martin and Marc Anthony. You may even find many mainstream artists who recorded Latin music when they wanted to spice things up. Didn't Steve and Eydie sing songs for Latin lovers or something?

ENTERTAINMENT

Besides socializing over food and drinks, roll up the rugs and start dancing. We're telling you, there is nothing sexier than Latin music. You may as well take advantage of that.

> This whole evening is about Havana when Hemingway lived there, when high stakes players—cloaked in discretion and good taste—filled the casinos, when Americans found the exotic right off their own coast. It's the Havana of Ricky Ricardo. And may we just say, when your guests hear the music and feel the rhythm, you won't have to 'splain nothin'!

Magical Mystery Party

Most folks wouldn't seek the company of someone who "dabbles in the occult." Instead, a lot of people would swiftly and quietly head for the nearest exit.

But then we got to thinking: Since the word *occult* means "unknown," as far as we're concerned, trigonometry falls into the category of occult. As does any chemistry equation you could toss our way, the procedure to fly a space shuttle, the composition of all matter, the proper steps to perform a quadruple bypass, and much more than we'd care to admit. So *occult* does not necessarily mean "creepy."

Come with us now, if you will, to a campsite on the edge of Budapest, where the last road meets with the forest. There we'll enter into the spirit of the occult, with its history, mystery, fringe (both tactile and lunatic), gypsies, palm readers, and tarot.

Through a veil of trees, a campfire is seen, and beyond it, colorfully painted wagons. The fire throws shadows of dancing men, women, and children dark of hair and light of foot. As you approach, you rustle the leaves underfoot, but the gypsies are not startled. You are expected. "Welcome, dear." With outstretched hands, they bring you into their world.

INVITATION

By Phone

"As the moon rises, the raven is on the wing. All things will be unveiled tonight at six, as we begin our Magical Mystery Party."

By E-Mail

As the moon rises, the raven is on the wing. All things will be unveiled tonight as we begin our Magical Mystery Party at 6:00.

Please consult your reader and let Joneen know if it's in the cards for you to attend.

MENU

We've designed a menu that is heavy (we don't use that term lightly!) in the tradition of Eastern European gypsies and fortunetellers. Use your good silver, mixed-and-matched tableware, and colorful linen tablecloths and napkins.

Food

You can easily prepare this menu in advance and freeze it.

- Goulash: A slow, all-day simmer in the slow cooker is simple and delicious. Serve alone or over egg noodles (the fat, flat kind, buttered to keep from sticking together) or white rice.
- Chicken *paprikash:* Same deal as the goulash.
- Sour cream for garnish
- Crusty French bread
- Apple pie and rum raisin ice cream
- Fortune cookies

Beverages

- Hearty red wine, such as a Burgundy or cabernet sauvignon
- Strong coffee with dessert
- Cognac or brandy after the meal

PROPS AND DÉCOR

- Gazing globe: We're sure someone in your neighborhood can lend you one. (See "Cynics Walk" on page 127.)
- Tiger Balm: It is said that rubbing this ointment into your "third eye" (the area just above the bridge of your nose) increases your psychic acuity.

- Tarot cards
- Votive candles for each place setting
- Candles set in coffee cans and Mason jars on the floor (Careful: Keep them out of walkways. You don't want to kick them over!)
- Low-lit lamps draped with scarves or diaphanous fabric
- Fabric hung in a doorway: You can easily accomplish this effect by draping gauze over a tension curtain rod affixed within the doorframe.
- Pillows
- Tambourines with streamers
- Fringed shawls: Wear them around the shoulders and around the waist.
- Chinese zodiac place mats: You should be able to get these at a Chinese restaurant. They should add another level to conversation as guests determine who was born in the Year of the Rat, the Year of the Snake, and other less savory years.

MUSIC

The trick here is to find that winning combination of frenzied, fast-paced music and compositions in minor keys.

- Violin music
- Squeeze box music
- Frantic Bohemian music
- Russian dance music

ENTERTAINMENT

As guests arrive, offer them drinks and get them in the mood for mystery. We advocate you center the action around your dinner table, allowing everyone to participate before, during, and after the meal. Here are some things that should keep you entertained:

- Palm lines: Search the library or Internet for illustrations of archetypal palm lines and their interpretations. Place a copy of them at each place setting. Pick up a few inexpensive magnifying glasses for better visual accuracy.

He: "Your love line splits!" She: "It does not!" He: "Well, it does too! Look right here—you can see where it veers off!" She: "It does not veer off!"

- Tarot cards: Purchase a few decks and follow the instructions that come with them.
- Ouija board: This one's always good for "You're moving it!" "Am not!" "Are too!"
- Horoscopes: Those little booklets from the grocery store are always handy, as are the horoscopes in your daily newspaper.
- Magic 8-Ball: It will answer your most pressing questions. "Oh, Magic 8-Ball, answer us now! Do the guests at this party give you any credibility whatsoever?" "BETTER NOT TELL YOU NOW."

How much of this magical mystery stuff is a reliable way to make one's decisions? Some swear by it, and we won't debate them. But let us give you an example of what happened when one of us consulted her horoscope before deciding to go out with one particular gentleman.

It was to be dinner at six, an outdoor concert at eight, and lakefront fireworks at ten. The little darling determined that all systems were go because her horoscope said the day would be a "10," the best rating possible. The information caused her to come up with some flimsy excuse to leave work early and sent her scurrying to buy a new outfit, which set her back half a month's salary.

That night, she was home by seven.

Bond, James Bond.

Schmidt. Harold Schmidt.

It doesn't quite have the same ring, does it? It lacks a certain panache. Nor does a bus trip to the Ho-Chunk Casino carry the same cachet as an evening at the baccarat table in Monte Carlo.

"Well, all we can afford is the bus trip to Ho-Chunk!" you whine.

Nonsense! With this party, you can create the elegance of a James Bond affair right in your own home. It won't be *the* Monte Carlo, but let it be *your* Monte Carlo. Come with us now, and enter the Bond Zone, full of champagne, martinis, tuxedos, evening gowns, cufflinks, thin cigars, diamonds, handsome men, beautiful women, high rollers, shooters, and players.

There's always room for a Bond girl at the gaming tables. Not only did the Bond girl have a strong figure, she was one as well. No mouse at the craps table, she! The Bond girl was smart, gutsy, and stunning—adjectives that will accurately describe each and every one of the female guests at your party, no doubt whatsoever. And oh, *James,* she'd prefer her martini on the dry side, if you please.

And the men—God love 'em—if this party can give them half the edge they fancy themselves having, by all means, let them posture away with their bellies sucked in. Get them all gussied up in those tuxes and then watch as they strut about like the demigods they surely are.

This party allows you to create a place for your guests where diamonds are forever, the martinis are cold, the gaming is hot, and the stakes are high. Best of all, an invisible current keeps players ready to roll twenty-four hours a day at a Monte Carlo casino, so the night is always young.

INVITATION

By Phone

"This is the concierge at *le Casino de Monte-Carlo*. Mr. Bond has arranged for your party to join him tonight for an interesting game of roulette at eight. Dress is formal, of course. May we tell him to expect you?"

By E-Mail

By Invitation Only: A place at the baccarat table has been reserved for you. Please contact the concierge at *le Casino de Monte-Carlo* by 5:00 P.M.

Ask for Schmidt. Harold Schmidt.

MENU

Everything is self-service. You'll have a table set up for food, so James can just walk over and help himself whenever he wants to nibble. Provide some high-quality paper napkins, and use your good china and silver.

Food

You'll be featuring hors d'oeuvres. Here are a few suggestions of the quick and easy variety:

- Shrimp platter from your grocer's deli
- Artichoke hearts on melba or cocktail rounds: Place an artichoke heart on a bread round. Cover with a mixture of equal parts mayonnaise and grated Parmesan. Pop under the broiler until brown. Garnish with a pimiento strip if you have time.
- Cheese and crackers
- Toast cutouts: You can use those playing-card cookie cutters if you really want to get cute. Serve with flavored cream cheeses.
- Mixed nuts
- York peppermint patties (These are a kick with martinis!)

Beverages

You'll be fine if you just have martini glasses, old-fashioned glasses, and wineglasses. If you have champagne glasses, bully. But James has too much class to sneer at you if you have to serve champagne in wineglasses, so don't worry about it. Have garnishes like lemon and lime peels, pearl onions, and stuffed olives cut up and available at the bar.

- Martinis—shaken, not stirred (*There.* We said it. And we're not sorry.)
- Champagne
- Sherry
- Crème de menthe over cracked ice
- Brandy, Scotch, or whiskey served on the rocks
- Liqueurs such as Drambuie, Kahlúa, Kalahari, and amaretto
- Wine

PROPS AND DÉCOR

- You'll have pockets of action set up throughout your party area. Use whatever is available, such as card or dining tables. And you'll need dice, cards, chips, plus the necessities that go along with each game, like that roulette wheel, for instance! Cover each gaming table with a white or green tablecloth.

- As with all our parties, lighting is key. Even if you have to borrow them from a friend, we want you to use small table lamps at each of your gaming stations. No overhead lighting! You can get plenty of that at the bingo hall.

- Dress is going to set the stage. We suggest you dress as formal as possible. Of course, we'd like to see the men in tuxedos, but if they can't do full-blown tuxes, how about faux tuxes? Have them put on black suits, white shirts, and black bow ties. The women can go as over the top as they want. If they want to be Bond girls, you just let them. Gracious, elegant, and stylish works well at any Monte Carlo casino.

MUSIC

- Smooth jazz, either contemporary or from the sixties
- James Bond soundtracks or a compilation of Bond theme songs (We *love* Tom Jones singing "Thunderball.")
- *Pink Panther* soundtracks
- Anything by Burt Bacharach
- An occasional bossa nova favorite to change the pulse of the room and get people moving

ENTERTAINMENT

- Want people to feel like high rollers without risking big money? When your guests come through the door, have them check in with a cashier, who will offer them Monopoly money. Or if you're playing with real money, have one-dollar bills available so people can break larger bills. However, if you want to play with big money, you can do that, too.
- Determine in advance who will be the dealers. You can take turns, or if people want to be dealers for the entire evening, you can station them at each table. If you're really going over the top, hire dealers.
- If you need a refresher course on the rules of the games, we suggest you pick up one of those little casino game paperbacks or *Hoyle's Rules of Games* at the library. Here are a few games people are likely to be familiar with:
  - Craps: Bet the pass line—shooter coming out. You can buy a felt craps table layout at a party store, or you can create your own by copying a craps layout from a book or web site. You will need a bumper of some sort surrounding your table, so if you have a huge box with sides approximately six inches high, it would work well. Fasten the craps layout inside the box, and you're golden. The dealer can use a squeegee to pull off the dice and chips.
  - Roulette: 'Round and 'round she goes. You can pick up a roulette wheel at a party or game store. We've even seen them at toy stores. If you're really inventive and motivated, you could fashion a roulette wheel out of a bicycle wheel—again, that's if you're feeling inventive and motivated.

- Blackjack: With that steely-eyed dealer showing an 8, do you dare hit that soft 17? In Monte Carlo, the house rarely loses. But this is your house, and the dealer could lose at any time and probably will.

- Baccarat: This is one of the most popular and elegant games. If we were really in Monte Carlo, you'd find us sidled up to Pierce Brosnan's James Bond as he tries to outwit the dealer. We'd be dripping in diamonds. Our waists would be tiny, our bosoms heaving, our gowns by Versace. When Pierce would draw us toward him to kiss our succulent lips for luck, a tiny bit of champagne would slosh over the glass and onto our manicured fingers, which Pierce would then take into his mouth, one by one, licking them and—*oh my! Where are our smelling salts!*

- International poker: Ten thousand dollars minimum entrance fee. The stakes are very high at this table, indeed. A place at the table in Monte Carlo is by invitation only, but what care you? You're sure to be invited tonight.

> We think you should offer a million-dollar jackpot tonight—with *real* money. Have the check all written out; just leave the name blank. The prize will go to the person who most closely resembles James Bond. That is, one million dollars to the guest who can
>
> - fly planes of any and all kinds;
> - maneuver powerboats at dangerous speeds;
> - ski while performing archery feats;
> - hang-glide into Red Square;
> - skydive with a bomb in one hand;
> - scuba-dive with a man-eater like a great white on one side and a man-eater like Ursula Andress on the other;
> - speak seven languages fluently;
> - always leave every one of his innumerable "tickle partners" happy;
> - gamble brilliantly and win enormous sums of money every time;
> - drink copious martinis while maintaining proper decorum and body weight.
>
> If your group of friends is anything like ours, we've no doubt it'll be a close contest.

The Marrakesh Express

This party is a departure in more ways than one. The Marrakesh Express will whisk you to a different time and place. Enter the world of fanciful intrigue. Escape to improvisation. Change your name and accent. Let your shawl slip off your shoulder and leave it there. Allow yourself to be won over by the sensuousness of eating with your fingers.

The best way to explain Marrakesh and this party's mood is by introducing an intriguing character: the American woman. She is the shadow against a Moorish arch on a narrow, amber-lit street. She is the faint scent of a clove cigarette. We encounter her in the colors of Morocco—terra cotta, russet, dark blue, sage green, and bright orange. We sense her in the languid *thunk-thunk-thunk* of an overhead fan. We hear her in the din of the marketplace by day and in the prayers chanted through a mist of spices at night.

The Marrakesh Express allows a dinner party to become an entire evening wrapped in imaginative sensuality. We hope your guests find themselves so caught up in the fancy of it all, that before the night is over, perhaps they'll even see her...the American woman.

INVITATION

By Phone

"Midge, this is Madge. Can you come for dinner tonight at eight? I'm planning an exotic evening in Marrakesh." If Midge inquires whether she can bring anything, a mysterious "just your hunger for adventure" should keep her sufficiently intrigued.

By E-Mail

A ticket has been purchased for you on the Marrakesh Express in the name of John and Mary Smith. Your reservations in the dining car are for 8:00 tonight.

Tickets can be retrieved at 123 Imagination Lane. Ring for confirmation.

MENU

If the age and agility of your guests allow it, serve this meal in traditional Middle Eastern style, which means on the floor. Use a very low table or place a board on a large ottoman and drape fabric over it. Use bed pillows wrapped in a sheet, couch cushions, or large floor pillows for seating. Have the food and drink within easy reach, so no one has to keep getting up and down. (Galvanized buckets work well for keeping cold beer and wine at your fingertips.) A nice touch prior to dining is to provide hot, wet cloths for guests to wash their hands.

Food

If you order out, you'll find a selection of great dishes at any Middle Eastern restaurant, deli, or caterer. But if you'll do the cooking yourself, keep reading. When choosing the dishes, remember that the flavors should reach "both ends of the tongue" with a nice balance of sweet and savory, fiery and cool. Here are some examples:

- Sliced, cold chicken: Whether you live in midtown Manhattan or rural North Dakota, we know you have access to those preseasoned, preroasted rotisserie chickens at grocery stores. What's not to love about them? Slice them up, squeeze a little lemon or lime juice over them, arrange them on a platter, and serve with some spicy dipping sauces. You can purchase the sauces or make them with plain yogurt, garlic, cumin, lemon, and a bit of red cayenne pepper.
- Warm pita bread
- Hummus
- *Baba ganouj*
- Yogurt-based cucumber salad
- Cold rice salad with dates, cashews, olive oil, lemon juice, and mint
- Salad with cabbage, apples, raisins, onions, and plum-vinegar dressing

- Grapes
- Ginger or coffee ice cream

Beverages

- Mint tea before the meal
- Mineral water with a lemon slice
- Beer
- Clean white wine
- Strong coffee after the meal

PROPS AND DÉCOR

- Set out anything woven, such as baskets or even place mats.
- Cover the floor with overlapping and askew rugs.
- Burn a stick of incense near the front door for when guests arrive (but make sure it doesn't interfere with those wonderful dinner smells later on).
- To transform your suburban two-story into a balcony apartment in Marrakesh, lighting is key. We want to see *lots* of candles: long, skinny, short, fat, knotted, polka-dotted, twisted, beaded, braided. The candlelight will create a fabulous ambiance, so don't skimp. When we gave this party, we filled the fireplace with candles. We'd even like to see you go so far as to use a bedroom lamp in the kitchen instead of that blinding overhead light.
- With a very large piece of fabric, mimic the look of a Bedouin tent over the area where you'll be doing most of the entertaining. You can use any type of fabric, but keep in mind the colors of Marrakesh. (Think fall palette.) Fasten clips or rings and a long piece of rope or twine to each corner of the fabric. Tie each of the lines to a hook, rail, picture nail—whatever is in the room—and adjust them until you have a loosely hung canopy. (If you have nothing to tie the lines to, you can purchase temporary sticky hooks that are guaranteed not to pull off your paint or paper.)

MUSIC

The library can help! Ask a librarian to set aside some Middle Eastern music for you. Otherwise, the following types of music will also work:

- *Alcantara: Arabo-Andalusian Voice—Morocco* by Amina Alaoui
- *Caverna Magica* by Andreas Vollenweider
- Oboe or flute selections
- Anything by Yanni
- New Age music

ENTERTAINMENT

- Enjoy all the novelties that the evening offers: the meal, the coffee, and your friends. Indeed, if you were really in Marrakesh, the entertainment might very well be nothing more than the lively art of conversation.

- If the spirit moves your guests as it did ours when we were in "Morroco," go ahead and dabble in a full-blown fantasy. We delighted ourselves and our guests with a game that was concocted right there on the spot: The American Woman. We fantasized about this woman of mystery and how we were connected to her. With a playful, imaginative group, you may go in and out of this fantasy all evening. One never knows what may happen on the Marrakesh Express! Here are some questions to inspire the imagination:

    - "Have you seen her yet.... the American woman? Some say she never laughs. Others say she never cries."

    - "They say the American woman has traveled all over the world. What stamps would the border guards see on her passport?"

    - "There's a precipice near the outskirts of Marrakesh. They say if you listen closely enough, you can hear the voice of every soul that ever fell in love with Morocco. What do you suppose those voices are trying to say?"

> As you watch your guests head down the walk at the end of the evening, you may catch a fleeting shadow out of the corner of your eye. And what was it that made the bushes rustle just now, almost imperceptibly? Was it the whisper of a breeze on this warm Moroccan night? Or was it the American woman?

¿Señora, Que Quiere?
A Party in Three Acts (Ladies Only!)

"Madame, what it is you desire?" Wouldn't that just be music to the ears of any woman? We happen to think this party is the ultimate gift to women from the men in their lives. Your husband and his friends—that is, the *houseboys*—will treat you and your lady friends to a day when responsibility flies completely out the window.*

This party is divided into three acts. Act I will take place in the afternoon as you gals lounge at a "resort." Right in your own back yard, you can become intoxicated by the coconut-oil scent of vacation. As you luxuriate in the sun, an hors d'oeuvres platter and a pitcher of margaritas will be brought to your fingertips.

Act II is the "girlfriendly" act of showering, changing, and becoming beautiful. (As you get older, Act II tends to take longer and longer.) There'll be hair to tame, bracelets to borrow, lips to gloss, and you may as well have fun doing it.

Act III will commence when the houseboys serve dinner then join you at the table, transforming back into the men of your dreams. After the meal, they'll offer coffee while you enjoy sexy Latin dance music.

With that understood, let us examine the question at hand: Madame, what *do* you desire? For one thing, you desire to be responsible for *nothing* and *no one,* if only for a day. You desire to capture that feeling of being at a Mexican resort. And you *seriously* desire to be waited on hand and foot by your houseboys, who will be willing to give massages, should you so desire.

Savor every moment. You deserve it, and he wouldn't have it any other way.

*Well, let's be realistic. Responsibility will *partially* fly out the window. As hostess, you'll need to take a few moments to set the plan in motion. First, get your husband on board. (It helps if you tell him the other husbands will pitch in, too.) Next, have him read this chapter so he knows what is expected of him. Finally, let him draw his own plan of action. (Just a thought: If he doesn't know mangoes from Manwich, you may want to offer a bit of guidance.)

INVITATION

By Phone

"Julie, Jeff has booked us on the most incredible all-inclusive package to Mexico! Can you be packed in a few hours?" She won't even be disappointed when you tell her it's not the *real* Mexico.

By E-Mail

Jeff has booked us on the most incredible all-inclusive package to Mexico!

Depart Anytown: 1:00 P.M.
Arrive Mexico: 1:05 P.M.

Depart Mexico: 9:00 P.M.
Arrive Anytown: 9:05 P.M.

Accommodations provided by the La Casita Tower, Resort, and Spa. Please telephone Ginny by 10:00 this morning to validate your reservations.

ACT I

MENU

You'll enjoy hors d'oeuvres throughout the afternoon. Since your houseboy knows where to find all the food, beverages, and serving pieces, turn him and the other fellas loose.

Food

- Sliced mangoes and papayas
- Guacamole with chopped fresh tomato
- White, blue, and yellow corn tortilla chips
- Refried bean dip with grated cheese
- Mango and jalapeño salsa

Beverages

Enjoy the drinks, but don't go wasting away in Margaritaville! While you may be tempted to overindulge, keep in mind that that would be like falling asleep during a massage.

- Iced Coronas with lime wedges
- Margaritas
- Lime slush
- Sangria: Combine wine (or nonalcoholic wine), club soda, melon balls, apples, oranges, lemons, and limes.

PROPS AND DÉCOR

- Lawn lounges (enough for all guests)
- Hammock
- Garden hose with misting attachment
- Big fluffy towels
- Boom box

MUSIC

The men should start the music as soon as guests arrive. Have them keep it loud enough to convince you that you're in a tropical paradise, but soft enough to allow for conversation. Here are some suggestions:

- Jungle and waterfall sounds: If you can get two boom boxes, play these CDs or cassettes simultaneously.
- Mexican poolside resort music, such as calypso and merengue

ENTERTAINMENT

- When the guests come through the door, the houseboys should offer towels, beverages, and hors d'oeuvres.
- As you lounge in the warm sun, the men can periodically offer a gentle misting or even a massage to any of you lovely *señoras*.

- You may wish to enjoy the sun in silence or perhaps you'll want to gab about the following topics:
  - "Men I Have Known"
  - "Choices I'm Glad I Made"
  - "Who Should Play Me in My Movie"
  - "If I Had a Million Dollars"
  - "Who My Mother *Should* Have Been"
  - "I Want Her Legs (or Cheekbones, Breasts, Fanny, and so on)"

ACT II

MENU

As you enter the bath and changing area, your guests will delight in the cool beverages and sweet treats the houseboys set up in advance. They'll really be delighted when they see that the men included napkins. (These don't need to be fancy. The fact that they remembered napkins is a gift in itself.)

Food

- Cold fruit platter: The men will have even included lemon and limes to squeeze over the fruit.
- Cantaloupe and mango slices drizzled with Tabasco and lime juice

Beverages

- Sparkling mineral water with a lemon wedge and cracked ice
- Lemonade

PROPS AND DÉCOR

- Moisturizers, powders, and body spritzers
- Fresh towels

MUSIC

- Jimmy Buffett
- Ricky Martin
- Frank Sinatra
- Tony Bennett

ENTERTAINMENT

This act is a little like that afternoon barbecue scene in *Gone with the Wind,* when the women traipse off to refresh themselves. Shower, style your hair, apply your makeup, do whatever it takes to become bewitching and beguiling. (Once your men get a load of you, frankly, they *will* give a damn!)

ACT III

MENU

While you and your gal pals get gussied up, the men will rearrange the lounge chairs and set up small tables for dining. The houseboys can lay out a buffet or serve dinner according to your instructions. Have them use fine linens and china or let them mix and match bright, colorful pieces.

Food

If you're going with takeout, here's when one of the houseboys will make a quick run to pick it up. If your houseboys are happy in the kitchen, they may want to put together these simple suggestions:

- *Quesadillas:* Your basic quesadilla recipe is to add grated cheese to a tortilla. Cook in a well-oiled skillet until the tortilla is browned and the cheese is melted. Cover with a second tortilla and flip to brown the other side. Garnish with a dollop of sour cream, guacamole, chopped tomatoes, and cilantro. Slice into wedges and serve. If you want to add variety, here are more suggestions for fillings you can add:
    - *Chipotle* chicken
    - Sautéed mushrooms with oregano

- Caramelized corn, zucchini, and Vidalia onion
- Grilled shrimp
- Chorizo

• Green salad: Toss assorted lettuces and herbs with a lemon vinaigrette.

Beverages

- Corona or Dos Equis served with a lime wedge
- Piña coladas
- Sangria
- Pitchers of ice water with citrus slices

PROPS AND DÉCOR

- White Italian lights for your shrubbery
- Candles
- Boom box

MUSIC

- Gipsy Kings
- Obo & Sol Luna
- Sexy Latin jazz

ENTERTAINMENT

- The men will light the candles and offer cocktails to get things rolling, then they will join you at your supper table.
- Sexy as that Latin dance music may be, we can think of no finer climax to the evening than for you to say good-bye to your guests, crawl into bed, kiss your husband good-night, roll over, and fall asleep.

> After attending this party, your guests may want to do it again as a round robin. The men will love this idea too, because every time they play houseboys, you women will owe them. (And we all know what *that* means.)

Parties That Get Ya Moving

Outdoor Summer Games for Big Kids

We were outside one fine summer day and saw someone strolling down our street, happily humming and singing to himself. The song was an oldie, and our wandering minstrel was singing, "If I could turn back the hands of time... If I could turn back the hands of time."

"Well, you can't," snapped that cynical voice inside each of our heads. But the very next second, our perfectly arched eyebrows shot up, and we were at it again.

We came up with a party that beautifully combines the person you *were* with person you've *become*. The party takes you to that juncture where your inner child meets your outer adult. It allows you to completely cut loose. Seriously, how many other adult activities do you know of that are this liberating but won't land you in the hoosegow or the doghouse the next morning?

We hosted this party when the lightning bugs and a full moon provided the only light, and we suggest you host yours at such a time, too. Many of these games are of the "sneak up and hide" variety, so if your head reflects a little more light these days, you may want to wear a dark cap.

INVITATIONS

By Phone

"Whatcha doin'? Come on over in about an hour! We're gonna play all those great outdoor summer games we played when we were kids! Wear something dark so no one sees you capturing the flag!"

By E-Mail

Ghost in the Graveyard! Run, Sheep, Run!

Here's your chance to steal the bacon, capture the flag, and have some fun! Show up at 7:00 tonight at 2020 Hindsight Street. Bug spray provided.

Call "Little Jimmy" by 5:00.

MENU

Just carry the refreshments out after the games. Enjoy coolers of beer, baskets of chips, and barrels of fun. Have another hour or so of cool-down, conversation, and diggin' the weather and company.

Food

- Chips and hot sauce
- Nibblies, such as crackers, pretzels, or nuts

Beverages

- Beer
- Soda
- Wine or wine coolers

PROPS AND DÉCOR

- Lawn chairs
- Picnic or patio table
- Citronella candles or torches
- Bug spray (You promised!)

MUSIC

If you have outdoor speakers, woolly bully for you! But if not, just carry out the boom box and find the oldies station. There's no need to get elaborate here.

ENTERTAINMENT

We're not going to tell you how to live your lives, but when we gave this party, the games went on no longer than an hour and a half. (We won't go on and on about backs and bones and our achin' bacon.) And let's be reasonable: You won't find that once-beloved game of Red Rover listed here. We're not ten years old anymore, and it's no longer sixty pounds of boy versus sixty pounds of girl. These days the fat-to-muscle ratio is a bit skewed, to say the least. Women have more fat (case in point: mammary glands) and men have more muscle; therefore, a one-hundred-twenty-pound soft body is no match for a two-hundred-pound hard body. So here are the games, and here are the rules. And for those of you who, as a kid, were chosen last or caught first, here's when you reap your revenge.

- **Ghost in the Graveyard:** The ghost is "it." Everyone scatters throughout the playing area. When we played this game, we used our entire neighborhood—both sides of the street. When the ghost tags a player, that player also becomes a ghost. So eventually, when someone comes tearing up to you as you're hiding behind a tree, you won't know if the person *is* a ghost or is *running from* the ghosts. We actually screamed while we played. The last person to keep from becoming a ghost wins.

- **I Spy:** The spy covers his eyes at the goal. After counting to a given number, he yells, "Here I come!" or "Oh God, I'm coming!" or whatever. He then tries to find other players. When he sees a player, he yells, "I spy Mary!" Both Mary and the spy race to the goal. Whoever gets there last is the spy for the next round. Play this till people get sick of it.

- **Capture the Flag:** Divide players into two teams and determine a playing area. This is especially fun if you can play throughout the neighborhood, as that allows you to sneak through yards, climb over fences, avoid dogs, and so on. Each team presides over half the playing area, and each keeps a "flag" (a washcloth, rag, T-shirt, bra, whatever) on its own territory. The objective is to capture the enemy team's flag and bring it to home territory. Players may go into enemy territory at whim to get the flag, but once in enemy territory, they can be tagged and put in the enemy stockade. They are "out" until a fellow team member tags them in the stockade. When one team brings home the enemy's flag, it's Miller Time.

- **Red Light, Green Light:** One person is the traffic light and everyone else is a car. The cars line up about twenty feet from the traffic light. The traffic light turns her back to the cars and yells "red light" or "green light." On green, as you may have already guessed, the cars can move forward. But without warning, the traffic light can yell "red light," at which point she whirls around quickly. Any cars she sees moving are sent back to the starting line. The first car to make it to the traffic light wins.

- **Run, Sheep, Run:** Players are divided into two teams, the hiders and the seekers. The seekers choose a captain. The seekers close their eyes and count to a given number while the hiders hide. When finished counting, the seekers try to find the hiders. When a seeker sees a hider, he notifies his captain, and the captain calls, "Run, sheep, run!" At that point, everyone races to a predetermined goal. The first player to reach the goal wins for her team. It's not a *baaaad* game (sorry, we just had to).

- **Pom-Pom Pullaway:** Draw two lines, one on each side of the playing area. The players stand on one line, and a tagger stands between the two lines. When the tagger yells, "Pom-pom pullaway!" everyone runs to the line on the opposite side. Whoever the tagger tags becomes a tagger also. It's sort of the way vampires work: Get bitten, and there *you* are, too. The last person to be tagged is the winner and is rewarded by becoming the first tagger for the next game.

- **Spud:** The players form a circle. Someone goes into the middle of the circle, throws a volleyball into the air, and yells someone's name, say, "Fred." Fred then has to catch the ball. The other players run from Fred until he yells, "Spud!" Fred stops dead in his tracks. The players stop dead in their tracks, too. The reason? So Fred can throw the ball at anyone he chooses! And he keeps right on throwing it till he misses! When Fred misses a target, he then begins the next round by throwing the ball into the air and yelling the name of another player.

- **The Boiler Burst:** Players stand in a circle around a storyteller. Mark each player's place with a chalk X or a stone. The storyteller, naturally, tells a story. Any kind of story. But at any given time, she inserts the words "the boiler burst." When these words are spoken, players are all to trade places, and the storyteller tries to steal one of their places. The person without a place now becomes the storyteller.

- **Light as a Feather, Stiff as a Board:** As kids, we were certain that we were witnessing some weird phenomenon when this game was successful. One person lies on his back on the ground. The others kneel around him, repeating the phrase "light as a feather, stiff as a board." Then using only their middle and index fingers, the players lift his body a few inches off the ground. Since we've pretty much all figured out by now that *ten people* usually have no trouble whatsoever lifting *one person,* the purpose of this game is pure nostalgia and ridiculousness.

- **Blind Man's Bluff:** Here's a chance for your guests to get a little naughty! Players gather in a circle with a blindfolded player in the center. The players circle around until the blind man calls "Stop!" The blind man then points his finger, and the player closest to where he's pointing moves into the circle. The blind man gets to be all touchy-feely to determine that player's identity. If the blind man guesses correctly, that player then becomes the blind man. If not, the blind man survives to grope another person.

> A bonus to this evening is that the games end when you're ready for them to end. Nobody's mom is making him come home as soon as it gets dark.

Hide-and-Seek in the Dark and on the Floor

Before you skip past this chapter, thinking, "Well, that may be fine for someone else, but Gordon and I don't do that kind of thing," ask yourself why Gordon and you wouldn't do this kind of thing.

Think of this party as an inoculation against fuddy-duddyism. Let us draw an analogy: If you'll be vacationing in South America, you may not relish the idea of getting the recommended vaccinations. But how does four days on the toilet sound instead? No question about it, when faced with the alternative, you get the shots! It's the same with life in general. If you don't step outside your comfort zone now, there will come a time when you won't be able to. With that in mind, humor us a little. Get down on all fours and play this game before it's too late!

May we share what happened when we hosted this party? Truth be told, we anticipated a bit of resistance from one of our guests. We thought he'd pooh-pooh us all over the place, but you know what? He didn't. The fact that it was our crazy idea and not his own was all the excuse he needed to let rip. After a few "Oh, you zany gals!" he dropped to hands and knees, and off he went. And wouldn't you know it? Before he left the house, *he* came up with an idea for "the next goofy thing we should do."

INVITATION

By Phone

(In a coy voice) "Ma-arge? *Tee hee*... George and I were wondering how open-minded you and Fred really are. Do you have a few hours to join us for something a little wacky tonight?"

By E-Mail

We'll count to ten, but don't make us wait.
We're playing games in the dark, so don't be late.

Call for details before 5:00 P.M. today!

MENU

We don't expect you to feed Olympic athletes, but provide something a little more substantial than pretzels and chips since your guests are such good sports. Make the food available buffet-style after the game. Use your everyday tableware and your everyday napkins.

Food

- Nachos: Get the prefried tostada shells and top with refried beans (combined with sour cream for spreadability) or a mixture of seasoned ground beef and beans. Grate Cheddar or Chihuahua cheese over the beans or meat. Top with jalapeños. Pop under the broiler until the cheese sizzles. Offer guests toppings like chopped tomatoes, green onions, black olives, and sour cream.
- Fritos Scoops! and salsa: Add a can of drained corn niblets or drained black beans and maybe even a bit of sour cream to a jar of store-bought salsa.

Beverages

- Margaritas: Pull out the blender or serve them on the rocks. Use the ready-to-go bottles of margarita mixes.
- Iced tea
- Seltzer water with lemon or lime wedges
- Beer: Since tonight's all about moving the herd outside the ol' comfort corral, let the beer reflect that, too, and get a brand or two you haven't tried before.

PROPS AND DÉCOR

The only things we're seeing here are kneepads or sweatpants. If you have extra pairs of either, have them handy in case Marge arrives all gussied up and expects something other than hide-and-seek.

MUSIC

You'll have a lot of latitude with music, but keep it light and fun, like the rest of the evening. Any tunes by these artists will fit the bill:

- Blood, Sweat and Tears
- Blues Traveler
- Brian Wilson

ENTERTAINMENT

- Determine the playing field. If areas are off-limits, let it be known ahead of time. To ensure safety, clear clutter and small furniture. When we played, we used the entire house. We had people hiding in closets, beds, under the couch cushions, in the bathtub. Screaming was rampant.

- When you decide it's time to play, extinguish all the lights. The seeker goes into a designated area and counts to a given number. The rest hide. When the seeker reaches her predetermined number and calls out, "Here I come!" a-comin' she is. And on all fours. Why, you ask? Confining players to their hands and knees is not only novel but it also slows everyone down. There's less chance of getting hurt if everyone is crawling along rather than running blindly in the dark.

- Make up the rules as you go along, if you like. When the seeker finds a hider, the former prey can become a hunter, too. Merry pranksters are welcome to toss items to throw the seeker off the trail.

- We don't recommend playing longer than forty-five minutes, as it does get a bit hard on the knees. Forty-five minutes will give you three good rounds. But your guests will decide when they've had enough. If they balk in a half-hour, keep in mind that ya gotta know when to hold 'em and know when to fold 'em.

- There is no point to this game, so don't go looking for one. It's pure goofiness.

> How many other parties offer you the chance to change the lives of your guests after a mere forty-five minutes? With this party, you'll infuse your friends with a taste for the madcap, and you'll never know where they will take it next. Like our formerly staid friend, your own friends may try to outdo you and invite you over for God-knows-what!

Pool (Swimming)

What is it about light reflecting off water that sends the imagination into overdrive?

Listen to this: Last summer at a friend's poolside barbecue, we found ourselves staying longer than the rest of the guests. With evening falling upon us, our host set out some lights. Simply by arranging the lights near the pool, the evening was transformed. The lights reflecting in the water did for the evening what David Niven did for the tuxedo. We recognized that inspired look on each other's face and began thinking about our next party. Watching those little lights twinkle, we realized we could just as easily have been at an embassy party in an exotic foreign country (maybe one that's even a little *dangerous!*). With that settled, our imaginations had their way with us, and we went along for the ride.

The ambassador's office calls, requesting we join their group for a spur-of-the-moment cocktail party around the pool. We spend the afternoon swimming, sunning, and inhaling the scents of suntan oil, fruity white wine, and lime. Late afternoon takes us to the poolside cabanas, where we slip into something linen and sleeveless. Our tanned legs look a mile long in strappy sandals. As dusk falls, white Italian lights are lit in the tropical foliage, and the reflections of tiki torches dance on the pool. A white-jacketed waiter offers another gin and tonic as the buffet is unveiled. A four-piece jazz combo plays something sultry, and despite the fact that everything around us is foreign, someone whispers that we are surely the most exotic creatures at the party.

Well! With all this inspiration pent up with nowhere to go, we had no choice but to host this party. When *you* host this party, there's no telling where your imagination will lead. This might be just the chance to impress that old flame. Be you male or female, there is simply no better light to be seen in than this.

INVITATION

By Phone

"Tim and I are having people at the pool today. We'll swim and sun in the afternoon. A light buffet will be followed by dancing, so bring what you'll need to stay on into the evening."

By E-Mail

You are invited to a pool party today.
We'll swim and sun in the afternoon.
A light buffet will be served in the evening, followed by dancing.

Call Alison before 11:00.

MENU

We suggest using unbreakable, colorful glasses and plates. However, use your best linens and silverware to make this affair elegant.

Food

- Assemble panini sandwiches on foccacia or sourdough bread in advance. Just before serving, brown them on a low-flame grill, then cut them into finger sandwiches. If you prefer not to make these, ask your favorite deli to make them. Here are some suggestions:
    - Chicken paninis—sliced chicken breast, mozzarella, red onions, tomatoes, fresh basil, chopped jalapeños, and mayonnaise
    - Ham paninis—prosciutto, fresh basil, red onions, Monterey jack, and tomatoes
    - Vegetarian paninis—roasted red peppers, artichoke hearts, black olives, tomatoes, fresh spinach, and mozzarella
- Sliced tomatoes drizzled with olive oil and served with fresh basil and slices of mozzarella
- Sliced Granny Smith apples with a squeeze of lime juice
- Gelato (Italian ice) for dessert

Beverages

- *Campari* and club soda on the rocks with lemon or lime
- Gin and tonic
- Vodka tonic
- Kir: Swirl a bit of crème de cassis inside a wineglass and add club soda and white wine.
- White wine spritzer with a lime wedge

PROPS AND DÉCOR

- Provide shade from sunlight. Perhaps an umbrella table will do the trick.
- Après swimming, have fresh towels and toiletries, such as shampoo and moisturizer, available in the showering and changing rooms. Perhaps even supply a bottle of aspirin in case anyone has a sun headache. If you *really* want to be thoughtful, provide glasses and a pitcher of ice water in the changing area.
- It's great if you have plants surrounding the pool to hold white Italian lights. But if you don't, use freestanding candle lanterns and tiki torches. Also, hang additional lighting a slight distance from the pool to make it seem as if the party area is larger.
- Hang small, three-tiered vegetable and fruit baskets from the outer branches of trees. Place a small glass container with a candle set in sand on each tier.
- As the waters still in the evening, what could be lovelier than floating candles in the pool?

MUSIC

- In the afternoon, delight your guests with beach or tropical music:
    - The Beach Boys
    - Bob Marley
    - Jimmy Cliff
    - Jimmy Buffett

- But when dusk arrives, go with something altogether sexy and sultry. We like music by the following artists:
  - Dinah Washington
  - Frank Sinatra
  - Michel Legrand
  - Andre Previn
  - k.d. lang
  - Herbie Mann
  - Stan Getz

ENTERTAINMENT

In the afternoon, you'll swim and sun, and come evening, you'll enjoy cocktails, dining, and dancing. The atmosphere may well keep the energy aloft till the wee hours of the morning.

> Surely you, too, have felt the intoxicating effects of a warm breeze, a low-slung moon, and lights reflecting off water. When *sultry* refers as much to the music as it does to the air, your party has the ingredients of a loaded cocktail.

Pool (Pocket)
A Party in Three Acts (Men Only!)

Gentlemen, start your engines, because this chapter is for you. This party is the flip side of our "ladies only" party (see "*¿Señora, Que Quiere?*" on page 44), because try as we might, we could not figure any way to get women interested in it.

First and foremost, forgive our impertinence, but we're curious as to the chicken-or-egg nature of those pool hall double-entendres: *pocket pool* and *scratching*. We're hip to that kind of guy talk. But which came first, the terms as they apply to sports or the terms as they apply to shorts? Okay, now that we got *that* out of our systems, we can move on.

You guys can't deny that you are as social as the rest of us in the pack, right? You find it pleasant to get together with friends. You enjoy looking like a shooter in your crowd. But unless you're a professional caterer, the chances of you putting together something that we'd actually call a party are slim. These are not sexist comments; we came to this conclusion by analyzing our own statistics. Polling the men we knew, only one hand went up when we asked, "Have you ever put together—completely on your own—a party for your friends?" And that singular gentleman declared his claim to fame to be one frat party in 1971. (He added this sheepish disclaimer: "You woulda hated it.")

Now's your chance to have a little get-together for the guys. And we'll show how to do it with one hand tied behind your back. It's divided into three easy acts: First you shoot some pool, then you grill some grub, and finally you enjoy the game. You don't need us to tell you how to hang out at a pool hall or kick back and watch your favorite team. But we will give you some tips so you *(yes, you!)* can make dinner for yourself and the gang.

Don't worry. Male bonding will abound. There's nothing pansy-pooh about this party. In fact, don't even call it a *party* if that makes you happier.

INVITATION

By Phone

"Bob! Wanna shoot some pool tomorrow and then come on over for steaks and the game?"

By E-Mail

Bob,

Any interest in shooting some pool tomorrow and then coming by for steaks and the game?

Call me—Lane.

MENU

You don't even have to *think* about a menu at the pool hall. But once you get to home base, you'll not only have to consider a menu, you'll also have to consider how you're going to serve it. Oh, come on! Move to the dining room! Surely, men can sit at the table and eat a regular meal even though no women are present! No good can come of trying to balance a plate on your knees while sitting in front of the TV. We think it'd be nice if you used real plates and silverware, but we're not going to come after you with fangs bared if you go with paper plates. We are aware that there is great sensitivity to girlie-man behavior when it's just the guys, and you may be ribbed into the next county if you were to pull out linen napkins, so use paper towels instead.

Food

So what's for dinner? Here are some suggestions:

- Steaks: Season with Montreal steak seasoning and barbecue on the grill. Grab the A.1. Steak Sauce and horseradish.
- Baked potatoes: Pierce then microwave. Serve with butter and sour cream.
- Corn: We know this is the only vegetable some men will eat. You can buy corn on the cob in the frozen food section, and all you have to do is microwave it. Make sure you have softened butter.

- Lasagna from the frozen food section, pretossed salad from the produce section, and garlic bread from the bakery section
- Chocolate layer cake from the bakery section
- Pizza if the other suggestions overwhelm you

Well, look at that! You just made dinner! When the game begins in Act III, microwave some popcorn or pull out some pretzels, nuts, corn chips, potato chips, what have you. But you didn't need us to tell you that.

Beverages

In Act I, you'll likely have a few drinks at the pool hall, sports bar, or home of someone who has a pool table. (Don't load up though. Since we feel it's our mission to always remind people not to drink and drive, we'll do it here, too.) But when you get to Act II, think about serving these drinks with your meal:

- Heavy red wine: Bordeaux would be *primo* with those steaks or lasagna, don't you think?
- Beer
- Soda

PROPS AND DÉCOR

Yes, that's right! Pull out those pink parasols left over from your wife's baby shower. Or do nothing. Then again, a little atmosphere never hurt anyone. You don't have to light candles or anything, but at least turn the lights down from interrogation level.

MUSIC

Boys, we don't even feel we have the authority to make any suggestions when it comes to music. But here are some artists that a few guys have said they wouldn't mind listening to:

- The Moody Blues
- Steely Dan
- Blood, Sweat and Tears
- Pink Floyd
- The Eagles
- Dire Straits
- David Bowie
- Counting Crows

- The Grateful Dead
- Matchbox Twenty
- Chicago
- Van Morrison

ENTERTAINMENT

- Act I: Shoot a few games of pool and have a few beers.
- Act II: It's back to your place where you'll fire up the barbie and have a tasty and substantial dinner. Enjoy one another's company. We have absolutely no idea what you men talk about when you get together. Part of us wants to know, yet another part of us remains steadfast in the belief that we probably think more highly of you in our ignorance.
- Act III: Switch on the game. You know, one consideration here: If Guy X gets this thing together and Guy Y happens to have a big-screen TV, you may decide to haul the stuff over to Guy Y's house.
- And that's it. No games. No "If I could do it all over again I would have…" touchy-feely activities. No group hugging. When the manly stuff comes to an end, real men just leave.

> The guys will likely leave your house without thanking you, and that's probably fine with you. The more awkward and uncomfortable they act when they leave, the better time they had. If they were to say anything nice, they'd be just one step away from getting gushy, and that's not a chance they're about to take. If they tell you your cooking sucks, never has a greater compliment been paid.

Hans Brinker, or The Silver Skates

Some of us take to winter like polar bears to ice. Others of us do not go gently into that good night and have to be dragged, kicking and screaming, every year out into the cold. For one of us, the distaste of winter can be traced back to a childhood trauma that the other of us finds so hysterically funny, she insists that it be included here.

To protect her privacy, we'll just call the subject of this story "Lulu." Lulu grew up on a Wisconsin farm that sat at the bottom of a steep hill. A gravel driveway ran up the hill, and each day the school bus would pick her up at the end of it.

This story takes place when Lulu was in sixth grade—a hard year by any standard. Let's just say Lulu was not a particularly attractive adolescent. We're talking blue, sparkly glasses, chubby-girl-size clothes, and a hairdo not unlike that of her sixty-year-old teacher.

The Monday following the Beatles' appearance on *The Ed Sullivan Show*, Wisconsin was hit with a ferocious ice storm. But in those days, unless there was a resurgence of the Ice Age itself, school was never called off. The waiting bus made a yellow splash against the monochromatic gray backdrop, and Lulu set out to run the five hundred feet up the driveway to the road. However, she soon discovered that not only was it impossible to run, it was equally impossible to *walk*. Down she went, spread-eagle on the ice like a newborn calf.

Now on all fours, Lulu caught on swiftly to the "hand-knee-foot, hand-knee-foot" method of body propulsion. In this fashion, she crawled, grabbing onto the occasional godsend (a piece of gravel) poking through the ice. The bus, still poised at the summit, was not giving up on Lulu and neither was she. Her exertion made her glasses steam up, and Lulu could only see over the top of them.

But even with her nearsightedness, she could not miss the open mouths on the faces now plastered against the bus windows. Making her way, Lulu lost all sense of time. The only sound was the stillness of the cold. That is, until the door of the bus finally opened. Then, shattering the silence, came shrieking and screaming, the likes of which she had not heard since…well, since the previous night on *Ed Sullivan,* actually.

In honor of Lulu, we created this party to prove that we can be the conquerors of our own environments. If we have to contend with ice and snow for at least three months out of every year, let's figure a way to make doing so fun.

INVITATION

By Phone

You may have to be sneaky if you have friends like Lulu, so try this:

YOU: Hey, why don't you come over this evening for some corn chowder and hot mulled wine!
THEY: Why, we'd *love* to!
YOU: Great! But there's something we're going to do first! [*And here the cobra strikes!*] We're going outside for some winter fun, and then we'll come back to the house to warm up!

By E-Mail

URGENT TELEGRAM!

Hans Brinker in town one day only. Stop. Has agreed to exchange famous "Dutch corn chowder" and "Dutch mulled wine" for afternoon of [sledding/skating/tobogganing]. Stop. Hans to present Silver Skates Award to participant bringing most ridiculous mode of snow transportation. Stop. Call Hans's agent, Tom, for snow conditions by 2:00 P.M. End.

MENU

When you return from an afternoon of winter fun, you'll want to warm your guests from the inside out. Allow your guests to serve themselves right from the kettle or the pot. It doesn't get any better or easier than hot off the stove. Provide the necessary ladles, spoons, mugs, and bowls. (Here's the chance to use that set of twelve onion soup bowls you simply *had* to have.)

Food

- Hans Brinker's Dutch Corn Chowder or Dutch Chili: We're kidding about these being Hans Brinker's, of course. They're not even Dutch, for crying out loud. You're on your own for the chili, but we're happy to provide you the fastest corn chowder recipe known to humankind: Mix 2 cans cream of potato soup (not the condensed kind) and 2 cans creamed corn. Add pepper, onion flakes, garlic powder, paprika, and dash of nutmeg.

- Crusty bread or croutons: Hot dog and hamburger buns will work. (We hate to admit it, but we've done this, so you may as well, too. If you're in a pinch, of course.) Spread on a thin layer of butter and sprinkle on some Italian seasoning. Pop them under the broiler until they're lightly browned and crispy. The trick is to cut them into small rectangles (like finger sandwiches) or even smaller squares (like croutons) to float on the chowder. Just don't serve them in the shape of a wiener.

Beverages

- Poor Man's Hot Mulled Wine: Combine cranberry juice, Burgundy or merlot, thin slices of citrus fruit, cinnamon, cloves, and allspice. Heat on the stove, simmer in the slow cooker, or zap in the microwave.

PROPS AND DÉCOR

- For snow activities you'll need the following:
  - Sledding equipment: Don't just use sleds, toboggans, and saucers. Get creative! Use inflatable pool toys, air mattresses, inner tubes (what are they, all of four dollars?), garbage bags, fannies!
  - Skates: We're sorry, but from what we see on televised skating competitions these days, we feel ripped off. Now they make skates with lamb's wool lining! Maybe we *all* coulda been a contenduh if our skates had been lined with lamb's wool when we were growing up! But by all means, rent or buy used skates before you get new ones for this party.
  - Cross-country skis: This is an option if most of your friends already own the equipment or if cross-country skis are easy to rent.

- Après snow, you'll need these items:
  - Electric blankets
  - Quilts and pillows
  - Candles or a fire in the fireplace

MUSIC

Whatever music you choose, make sure it suggests "comfort following the cold"—that is, make it the musical equivalent of macaroni and cheese. For us that happens to be big band: Glenn Miller, Harry Connick, Jr., Tommy Dorsey, et al. You know your guests better than we do, but once twilight envelops you and you're mellow from the wine, make sure the music keeps that feeling going.

ENTERTAINMENT

- There's four new inches of fresh, powdery snow, the sun is shining, and it's relatively warm. No forty-below temps, no wind chill to speak of, no gray, drizzling sky. Take advantage of this gift from above!
  - Sledding: We're talking this one up because it's really the easiest to get everyone to agree on. The only thing funnier than watching someone sled down the hill is watching him trudge back up. Or how about this scenario: Everyone wants the same sledding apparatus only to find out after one run that it doesn't work very well. It's not long before you hear people trying to ditch the now-discovered-to-be-sticky blue saucer: "Joanie, *you* can have the blue one now."
  - Skating: From Sonja to Tanya, do we even dare attempt to teach one another some of the fancy moves? Do any of us really know how to do a triple Salchow? (No.) How daring you get will be up to you, but the only advice we have when it comes to skating is that you make sure it's safe before you step onto the ice.
- Once you're back inside, warm up to room temperature with a few games under electric blankets or quilts. Play till the chowder and mulled wine are ready!
  - Bundle Bug Boogie: Adolescent? Naturally, since we just made it up. Fun? We think so. It's merely a silly "guess whose feet are touching yours" kind

71

of game. Size may not matter here, but flexibility does. (Just don't touch anything that's not wearing a sock!)

- Snowball Fight: Tear out a sheet of notebook paper for each guest. On each sheet, write the name of a guest and a stunt you'd like him or her to perform. Crumple the sheets into balls. While still under the blankets, start a snowball fight. When the timer sounds to end the round, whoever has the most snowballs picks one, opens it, and reads the name of the guest and the stunt. (For example, "Andy has to sing a rendition of 'Second Hand Rose.'") Keep playing until the soup is hot and the wine is served or until people start balking.

> We don't know about you, but when we were kids and read *Hans Brinker, or The Silver Skates*, we found the title very curious. If the author couldn't decide what the title should be, how are we to decide? What we did decide, however, was to give our winter outdoor party the same name. And may Hans Brinker put the "win" back into winter for us all!

We're Rollin'!

We have some friends who own their own plane. It's a sweet little Cessna, and they, along with other pilot friends, formed a group called the Lunchwaffe. The Lunchwaffe regularly flies to nearby cities to have lunch, dinner, or whatever. "We're always looking for excuses to fly our plane," our friends admitted. "The focus of the outings is more the journey than the destination."

Okay, we admit it. We were jealous. Sure, we thought, wouldn't we all like to own our own planes and go flying off at the drop of a hat! But before the green-eyed monster completely overtook us, we decided we'd come up with our own variation of the Lunchwaffe. Getting there could be half the fun for us, too, even though we were confined to land!

So what you're reading now is a party for those of us who don't own planes—never mind that we're not brave enough to get pilot's licenses anyway. The idea of this party is to go on an outing with friends, using any mode of transportation other than a car. How creative you get will depend on the modes of transportation available in your area. But we happen to think it'll be an enjoyable challenge for anyone to plan how to get from Point A to B to C and beyond. In fact, the more odd and unusual the mode of transportation is, the more fun you'll have.

INVITATION

By Phone

"Joanne, let's get the heck outta Dodge. There's a stage leaving this evening at five." (Who knows? Maybe you'll mean that literally!)

By E-Mail

There's a stage leaving this evening at 5:00.
Let's be on it, and get the heck outta Dodge.

Call Peter for details.

MENU

While your destination may well be a restaurant, we're going to provide you with a quick, easy, and portable picnic. If you want to schedule a stop at a liquor store or deli, you can easily pick something up en route as well. To transport food and beverages, place them and a cold pack in a brown bag and then carry the bag in a backpack. Include disposable cups, napkins, small plates, and plastic forks. You know what would be *really* fun? You'd have to check ahead of time, but it would be a hoot to have your picnic right on board a train, provided the ride was long enough. There's something completely decadent about popping open a bottle of champagne on a train. Wherever you end up eating, here's a menu that's simple and fast.

Food

- Sub sandwiches: Stop at a sub shop and pick up a sandwich for each guest. Find something relatively generic, such as cold-cut combos or Italian subs, and get the fixings and condiments on the side. That way, you don't have to remember that Sheila doesn't want olives or that Vince hates onions.
- Cold fried chicken: Don't forget to bring a saltshaker! "You simply can't have cold fried chicken without salt" is one of our favorite mottoes.
- Cold couscous salad: Add olive oil and balsamic vinegar dressing. Top with chopped veggies, such as roasted red pepper, sautéed zucchini, black olives, and green onions.
- Cold tortellini or ravioli salad: Toss with caesar dressing and add freshly chopped basil.
- Potato salad
- Cold shrimp: Marinate in oil, vinegar, oregano, lime, cilantro, salt, and pepper.
- Seasoned breadsticks
- Olives
- Empire apples (what God intended apples to be): Slice then dip in peanut butter and roll in sunflower seeds.
- Brownies

Beverages

Pack a Thermos with your favorite drink or one of these suggestions:

- Daiquiris
- Iced tea
- Lemonade or slush
- Hot cocoa or flavored coffee
- Champagne (Well, maybe not in a Thermos.)

PROPS AND DÉCOR

You'll need to be armed with public transportation schedules, if that's your chosen mode of transportation.

MUSIC

If possible, bring the boom box and find a radio station everyone can agree on. Otherwise just enjoy the music your mode of transportation makes, be it the *chuga-chuga* of a train or the *clip-clop* of a horse and carriage.

ENTERTAINMENT

- Visiting a park or forest preserve would be fun.
- If you're heading into town, plan the evening around visiting a gallery, taking in a concert, or going to a movie.
- Maybe you won't even have a destination in mind. Maybe you'll just see where the transportation takes you. The point here is not the destination, but the journey. (You may have heard that one before.)
- Don't forget that you also have to get *back,* so plan accordingly.
- We came up with a variety of transportation modes that will keep you out of your car. (Parking rates are highway robbery, anyway—another great selling-feature of this outing.) Use any of these or a combination thereof, and get rollin'!

    - Bus
    - Train
    - Ferry
    - Tourmobile

- Streetcar
- Trolley
- Historic trolleys
- Water taxi
- Horse and carriage
- Bicycle
- Horseback
- Boat
- Roller or in-line skates
- On foot

- And, of course, if you have that real good friend who just happens to have an airplane, be nice to him.

> Our friends got completely into this party because we planned a fantasy scenario around it. Mind you, fantasy play is not necessary, but here's what we concocted. Courtesy of our imaginations, we weren't taking the train into Chicago, we were taking the train into the heart of East Berlin, where we were spies. *Glamorous* spies. Once there, we would meet with our Cold War allies. The future of the free world was at stake, and somehow we needed to slip across the border undetected. As in all our fantasies, we were gorgeous, witty, brilliant. No one on the train could take their eyes off us, but we were unable to discern whether it was because they suspected our mission or because of our breathtaking beauty. Oh, did we happen to mention what we were wearing? Well, it wasn't much. And that's all we're going to say about that.

Any Given Sunday

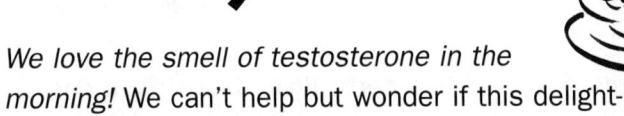

We love the smell of testosterone in the morning! We can't help but wonder if this delightful little hormone is what gives sports fans such incredible drive. Testosterone incites a palpable fever pitch when competitors go for fourth and goal with ten seconds on the clock or even when competitors go for that last corned beef on rye sitting on the buffet table.

Sports and sandwiches go hand in hand. So here's the game plan: You round up the gang for football, basketball, volleyball, or whatever. Afterward, the *sportifs* return to your house to enjoy tremendous sandwiches while going over the postgame wrap-up.

Read on and learn how to make your games and sandwiches something to cheer about. *We love the smell of corned beef on rye after a game!*

INVITATION

By Phone

"Why, Jimmy, you big, strapping, bulging hunk of solid muscle and bone, you! How would you like to come over for a few hours tomorrow and demonstrate your athletic prowess to the rest of the gang?" Mention the sandwiches, and he'll be practically on your doorstep.

By E-Mail

Tryouts for the U.S. Olympic Team to be held on Sunday.
Qualifying rounds for volleyball begin at 10:00 A.M.
Sandwiches will follow 12:00–2:00 P.M.

Please call Kurt at the Olympic Village.

MENU

Either guests can make their own sandwiches or you could make them the night before and keep them refrigerated. Wrap them in butcher paper and tie them with string. That way, they're easily portable in a basket, bucket, or tray, and you're free to enjoy the activities with guests. (Plus, it lets the dressings moisten the bread.) Serve on colorful paper or plastic plates and provide colorful paper napkins.

Food

As the sandwiches play an enormous part of this party, if you have to cut corners, don't let it be here. Find a good bakery and deli, and pick up an abundance of wonderful breads, meats, and cheeses. May we suggest you make sure you have enough so each person can have two generous sandwiches? In addition to ketchup, mustard, and mayo, have some spicy condiments available, such as *gardiniera, pepperoncini,* and hot pepper flakes. Here are a few quick and easy sandwich ideas:

- Roast beef and red onion with horseradish and Dijon mustard on potato bread
- Chicken salad with lettuce and tomato on whole-grain bread
- Corned beef and Swiss with mustard on rye
- Sub sandwiches: Cold cuts and veggies with oil and vinegar dressing on French rolls
- Avocado, Monterey jack, ripe olives, tomatoes, greens, and sprouts with cucumber yogurt and garlic dressing on pita
- Open-faced cream cheese and watercress on whole-grain bread
- Open-faced chipped beef, cream cheese, and chopped green onion on rye
- Turkey and shredded smoked Gouda with tomato, lettuce, and mayo on wheat
- Muffuletta: Cotto salami with prosciutto, provolone, and olive salad served on a hard French roll

You might consider serving a few side dishes as well. Here are some examples:

- Cole slaw with celery seed
- Carrot and raisin salad

- Chips and French onion dip
- Fritos and bean dip

Beverages
- Beer
- Wine
- Mineral water with a lime wedge
- Soda

PROPS AND DÉCOR

Make sure you have the proper equipment to play the sports of your choice. This includes anything from a Nerf football to a stable of horses. Even if you don't own all the equipment, your friends should be able to supply what you're missing.

MUSIC

Instead of listing any specific selections, let us suggest that you keep the music lively and keep that energy flowing. Or why not pull out your music collection and have the guests make the selections themselves?

ENTERTAINMENT

- Invite your friends to meet you wherever your activity will take place—the beach, riding stable, lake, school athletic field. Afterward, people will go to your place for the goods.
- Here are some of the athletic pursuits we've done with friends. We all came away thinking we were *enormously* talented, of course.
    - Touch football
    - Baseball
    - Basketball
    - Horseshoes
    - Doubles tennis or badminton
    - Table tennis

- In-line hockey or broomball
- Bocce ball
- Shuffleboard
- Water polo (We love the idea of using underpants for headgear—they look the same!)
- Beach volleyball
- Boating, fishing, water-skiing
- Croquet
- Horseback riding

• Whether you choose to play for fun or profit, for an hour or an afternoon, these gatherings invariably invite cunning of one type or another. Take our monthly games of basketball, for example. We women got sick of the men always hogging the ball, so we decided to make new teams so it was guys versus gals. But then our height and weight put us at a disadvantage. How we evened the playing field was nothing short of female ingenuity at its best. Knowing our opponents' greatest weakness, we thought it natural to strike there. And *natural* we were. You should have seen their faces when seven women emerged from the locker room wearing shorts and nothing else but Maidenform sports bras.

• When guests arrive at your home, either during or after the sandwiches, you may wish to enjoy a video. Perhaps a new release you missed at the theater? Or perhaps a classic sports movie like *The Longest Yard*? And if anyone whines about sore muscles and bucks for a massage...well, that's what friends are for.

> Oh, if we can just pass along one additional suggestion: If you're going to play, play *before* the sandwiches. Don't do it the other way around. Because once you bring out those delicious creations, that's probably going to put the kibosh on sports for the day.

Dining—Fine or Otherwise

Commune Dinner

How many communes do you think are in the United States today?

Our money's on none. But the question "Whatever happened to communes?" is not going to place us in the quandary that the centuries-old question "Whatever happened to dinosaurs?" has. We already have it figured out. Oh sure, communes started off with pipe dreams of peace, brotherly love, harmony, blah, blah, blah. Then people actually started *living* with one another. And we all know what happened then!

"Oh, he's so laid back" turned into "He has absolutely no ambition." "She's a complete free spirit" eventually translated into "She can't handle responsibility." "She just doesn't believe in those sexist divisions of labor" came to mean "She refuses to clean one single thing." "He makes me laugh all the time" morphed into "He's a one-trick pony, and I've heard all the jokes a hundred times already. I wish he'd shut up."

The seeds of disillusionment began to sprout in communal living as soon as the first bowl of lentil soup was finished and it was time to do the dishes. Two weeks in, and it was looking as though someone poured Miracle-Gro on those seeds of discord. Then it was good-bye to the Hog Farm.

With this said, the beauty of the communal dinner party is that you can achieve that earthy-crunchy feeling of peace, togetherness, and collective bread-breaking without actually having to live with your friends (who, by our calculations, would be your *former* friends if you did).

INVITATION

By Phone

"Alison, we want to break bread with you and Jason tonight. Can you come share with us?" (Be sure to get the word *share* in there somehow. That's one buzzword that was used ad nauseam when communes were in full swing.)

By E-Mail

We want to share a meal, peace, and harmony with you. Can you break bread with us tonight?

If you can join us for a Commune Dinner, call Sean before 5:00.

MENU

It's a peaceful, easy feeling at your table. We're even imagining someone's legs thrown over the corner of the table. The menu here is very simple, just like it was in communes. We tried to make it mostly vegetarian, but you'll notice we did sneak a little meat in there anyway for the carnivores among you. Be sure to provide big cloth napkins.

Food

- Soups: If you don't have all day to simmer a variety of soups, pick them up at a deli or look for the frozen kind. Here are some suggestions:
  - Navy bean
  - Lentil
  - Potato-Cheddar
  - Potato-leek
  - Cream of chicken
  - Spinach tortellini: This is so easy, we've included the recipe: In a pot, combine 2 large cans of whole tomatoes, 1 bag of fresh spinach, 1 package of cheese tortellini, and oregano to taste. Simmer for a half-hour, and it's soup.
- Hearth breads: Best if homebaked, otherwise hit the bakery. Maybe even get banana bread, cranberry corn bread, or lemon poppy seed bread. Serve with the following:
  - Honey butter
  - Herbed butters
  - Rhubarb, blackberry, and raspberry jams

- Salad: We'd like to see just about everything in this salad: chopped greens (romaine, iceberg, spinach, watercress, radicchio), chopped red cabbage, zucchini, diced apples, green onion, sunflower seeds, cubed cheese, raisins, and fresh basil. Serve with olive oil, balsamic vinegar, and homemade croutons. To make croutons quickly, spread bread with butter or olive oil, sprinkle on Italian seasonings, and brown under the broiler. Then cube and add to the salad. (Gee, we want some now!)
- Herbed tomato-cheese muffin crowns
- Big homemade (or as close to homemade as you can buy) cookies
    - Oatmeal raisin
    - Chocolate chip
    - Molasses

Beverages

- Pitchers of sangria
- Pitchers of ice water with orange slices
- Assortment of teas served in big mugs

PROPS AND DÉCOR

- Set a votive candle at each place setting and arrange a mass of different-size candles in the middle of the table.
- Display greenery clippings from your back yard or from the local grocery.
- As hostess, put on that peasant dress if you've got one.

MUSIC

Whatever you choose, it's gotta be mellow, and it's gotta have *meaning*. We could see any of the following working beautifully:

- New Age
- World music
- *Canyon Trilogy* by R. Carlos Nakai
- *Winds of Honor* by Gary Stroutsos

- *Black Sand* by Ledward Kaapana
- *Hawaiian Slack Key Guitar in the Real Old Style* by Keola Beamer
- Classical
- Anything by the following artists:
  - Peter, Paul and Mary
  - Donovan
  - The Association

ENTERTAINMENT

This party is mainly to have friends share (now *we're* saying it!) a meal. But if you want to add an activity or two that will incorporate a bit of "how well do you know each other?" we have couple of suggestions:

- At each place setting, include a pen and a pad of paper. Have each guest write two statements about him- or herself that are true and one that is false. The statements should be things the other guests would likely not know. Here's an example: 1) I once hitchhiked across Europe; 2) I had my picture taken with President Reagan; 3) I played tuba in the high-school marching band. Other guests then determine which is the false statement. Play for points or for fun, and play at least two or three rounds.
- Purchase an inexpensive white tablecloth and colored permanent markers, one or two for each guest. During dinner, invite guests to doodle, draw caricatures of themselves or of one another, or sum up their life philosophies in one sentence each.

> To more fully illustrate how the Commune Dinner is better than an actual commune, let us tell you what happened to a friend of ours. To protect his privacy, we'll call him "Ben Hadd." Circa 1970, Ben sold all his personal belongings, quit his job, gave his money to some swami in California, and left the Windy City for the swami's compound on the shores of the Pacific. However, upon his arrival, Ben discovered that his swami had split with the dough and was now hanging ten in Hawaii. Clearly, this idealistic theory didn't translate into reality. But the Commune Dinner is ideally and realistically nothing more than a down-to-earth dinner party with nary a swami, sanctimonious philosophy, or Earth Shoe in sight.

Done Yer Duty

Most of us have delightful memories of holiday warmth and togetherness. Well, some of us do. A few of us may recall one or two happy holiday memories—if pressed. The rest of us remember hearing stories about *other people's* happy holidays. Nevertheless, year after dogged year, every last one of us attempts to pull off some sort of Holiday Nirvana with the relatives.

We've all been there. Visions of sugarplums may have danced in our heads, but reality is usually more in line with this:

The faint scent of salve announces Grandma's arrival before she is even through the door. The candles have to be quickly snuffed because of her oxygen tank. While others scurry about, trying to make her holiday merry and bright, she plops her fanny into the easy chair in front of the Bears game and proceeds to eat an entire box of Poppycock before the final whistle sounds. Dinner is served, but there she sits, glued to the tube because now she's not hungry. And woe unto you if you pack away the leftovers after the meal—the old bird expects a doggie bag. And dear, if you could just put small amounts in separate containers, then she could freeze them for later. After all, it's just her now.

Yes, you willingly took on that sweet yoke again this year, and by the time the evening—or the week!—is over, you'll just as willingly cast it off. And when the moment of triumph arrives and they're out the door, before the lock even clicks in the tumbler you can be on the phone, inviting over friends who no doubt have been through the same thing. Let heaven and nature sing!

INVITATION

By phone or by e-mail, it's the same. The only difference is that you'll be singing it on the phone.

(Sing to the tune of the "Hallelujah Chorus" from Handel's *Messiah*.)

Hallelujah! Hallelujah!
They are gone now. We are happy. Our heels are in the air.
Hallelujah! Hallelujah!
There is cheese log. There is turkey. 'Nuff booze to sink a ship.
We did our part valiantly! Come and hail us!
Hallelujah! Hallelujah! Hallelujah! Hallelujah!

MENU

We're not even going to ask you to set a table. Just place your tableware in easy reach and let everyone have at it. We fully expect your newly liberated guests to hang around the kitchen, sit on the counter, hover around the stove, and compliment you on how clever you are with those leftovers.

Food

- Cheese fondue: If you don't have a fondue pot, melt that cheese log in the upper pan of a double boiler and add a little white wine and spices. Cube turkey, bread, and fruit and provide some forks or skewers. You can also use fresh veggies. (We're sure most of that holiday veggie tray remains untouched.)

- Curried turkey salad: Cube the turkey, add mayonnaise, celery, apples or grapes, and curry powder. Serve it on a bed of chopped lettuce. It's that simple.

- Potato pancakes: Using your hands, form your cold-from-the-fridge mashed potatoes into flat cakes. Press each cake into flavored bread crumbs and brown it in butter. Serve with applesauce, sour cream and chives, or ketchup. (Don't worry about the fat. It will help with the emotional and verbal constipation you've likely been experiencing.)

- Chocolate fondue: Use just the creams from that five-pound box of Fannie May Assorteds that Uncle Wilbur says "Christmas isn't Christmas" without. (You should be able to tell the difference between the creams and the jellies by checking out Grandma's poke-holes on the bottom of each chocolate.) Melt in a double boiler and serve with the following:
  - Bananas: You have enough to start your own Monkey Island because Dad *had* to keep his potassium levels up.
  - Oranges, apples, and pears: Make short work of that fruit basket. If you have time, marinate the pears in that sweet wine that came from a previously unheard-of Baltic region and ended up on your desk as a gift from the office.

- Upside-down pie à la mode: Scoop vanilla ice cream into a serving dish. Pour a little rum over it if you're feeling especially devilish! We're guessing you don't have too much pie left, but take what you do have and crumble it over the ice cream.

Beverages

- Mimosas: *They* always had to have plenty of orange juice at breakfast, and you still have plenty now. Add champagne to it.
- Blender drinks: The whir of the blender can sound like a giant sigh of relief after a week of making every kind of old-fashioned known to humankind.
- Snow Blowers: We just now made up the drink, but doesn't it sound good? Eggnog, ice, a little nutmeg, and way more rum than you used in the eggnog you served in those little cups. Whip them in the blender and serve them icy.
- Yukon Icon (We All Con!): This drink combines hot apple cider and Yukon Jack or your favorite whiskey. The proportions are up to you. Serve with a candy cane instead of the ubiquitous cinnamon stick.

PROPS AND DÉCOR

There's no disguising that seven-foot blue spruce in your living room, now is there? So turn off the room lights, turn on the tree lights, and enjoy the décor you've already got up. However, feel free to pack away those holiday Precious Moments figurines that Aunt Mildred keeps shoving at you. Like a terrier with a pants cuff, she will simply not let this tradition go, and every year you've gotten a new one. But once Aunt Mildred has left the building, these do not need be displayed any longer.

MUSIC

Here's something new and exciting: *You* get to pick the music! No more *Gatlin Brothers Country Christmas.* No more *Perry Como Yuletide Tunes.* No more *Tennessee Ernie Ford Sings Grandma's 100 Favorite Carols.* You want low-key, sedate, classical? It's yours. You want Smokey, the Temps, and the Tops? You got it, and no one's going to whine, "Oh, come on! Put on something more Christmas-y!"

ENTERTAINMENT

- Share your holiday war stories in a game of "Can You Top This?" As they say, smoke 'em if you got 'em, and you sure as heck do. Just make sure your guests realize this is meant to be in good fun. We'd hate to see this game get mean and ugly.

- When you're all relaxed and comfy, how about gathering around the tree to share memories of Christmas past? The time your sister saved up to buy you that sweater you wanted so much. The Christmas it began snowing just as you came downstairs in your pajamas before dawn, when Dad was already building a fire and Mom was already stuffing the turkey. When Grandma, God love her, brought over the warm-from-the-oven gingerbread men. Or when Aunt Mildred—oh, sweet dear that she is!—was there for your Christmas Eve church program when you were in third grade. You'll dab at your eyes before you're finished, and you'll find yourself wondering how you ever got annoyed at those dear people you call family. And so there you'll be. You'll unwittingly get yourself all primed for next year. (If that's the case, you may wish to hang on to this book.)

> Celebrate all the emotions and tradeoffs that come with being part of a family. Carry on till the yawns begin. Realize that the strange feeling you're experiencing is that of your headache being gone. Then unplug the tree lights, hit the sack, and sleep in heavenly peace.

Blue Plate Special

There's a phenomenon afoot that makes us crabby: the new use of the word *real*. In this time of self-exploration, being *real* has become the one-size-fits-all justification for just about any kind of shenanigans someone wants to pull, such as divorcing one's wife to start a *real* life with "Bambi" in Vegas. We've had our fill of this nonsense, and the only *real* we want is 2 O/E, hash browns w/ toast.

Let us introduce you to something real, as God intended the word *real* to mean. Art & Vi's Blue Plate, until it recently closed, was a neighborhood diner located on a busy corner in downtown Lombard, Illinois. The chrome-rimmed lunch counter was filled with regulars who never failed to make Art & Vi's a part of their day. Politically incorrect smoking was allowed (probably even encouraged!), fluorescent lighting glared overhead, and retirees hollered from one end of the counter to the other about local and national politics. While Vi manned the skillet, Art put out the orders, and the waitresses never stopped pouring coffee. Even the name *Blue Plate* sounds uncomplicated, don't you think? It's where the food isn't *haute*, it's just *hot*.

When Vi passed away, the place closed down, and the neighborhood really hasn't been the same. We miss it. With all of that in mind, we're going to help you re-create a breakfast diner in your own house. While you're at it, raise a coffee cup to Art and Vi, a real pair if ever there was one.

INVITATION

By Phone

"This is Jane of Jane's Blue Plate Diner. We're celebrating our grand opening tomorrow, and we'd be right pleased if you'd join us for breakfast at nine!"

By E-Mail

Announcing the opening of Jane's Blue Plate Diner!

We'd be right pleased if you'd join us for breakfast tomorrow morning! We start slingin' hash at 9:00!

Call Jane tonight!

MENU

Your very own Blue Plate Diner is a place where everyone gets to be a cook, everyone gets to be a server, and everyone gets to be a customer as well! You'll eat in shifts—half of the group acts as cooks and wait staff while the other half enjoys breakfast. The cooks and wait staff may linger over a cup of coffee with the customers before the shift change, at which time it'll be their turn to be served.

Food

Here's what we suggest for your menu:

- Eggs: Lots and lots and lots of them. The cooks should be prepared to fix these babies scrambled, over-easy, or sunny-side up.
- Tortilla scrambles: Tear up tortillas and brown them in butter. Add chopped green onion. Then toss in eggs seasoned with salt, pepper, and cumin. Scramble away and serve 'em hot.
- Toast: Do yourself a favor—butter bread in advance and pop it all under the broiler.
- Flapjacks, griddlecakes, or pancakes: Whatever you call them, make them in mass quantities and keep them warm in the oven.
- Warmed maple syrup
- Butter cut into pats and placed in bowls
- Bisquick biscuits
- Jellies and jams: Serve in small bowls with teaspoons.
- Bacon: Apple bacon, maple bacon, peppered bacon, or whatever bacon you have. Remember, there are no breakfast police, so go ahead and take advantage of the microwave.

- Sausage links
- Cinnamon rolls: Get the tube of dough that you open with a *thwack!* on the counter. Much as we'd love the Pillsbury Doughboy to pop out, he never does. But even so, these rolls are yummy, and they smell wonderful. (Be advised, however, that their shelf life can be measured in minutes, so serve them right from the oven.)

Beverages

- Fresh orange, grapefruit, and tomato juice
- Coffee: Use a large insulated decanter to keep your supply hot, fresh, and plentiful.
- Real cream: Serve in small pitchers, if you have them.

PROPS AND DÉCOR

No diner is complete without the following:

- Aprons
- Yellow pencils
- Note pads
- Homemade name tags for the servers
- A wire strung across your cooking area
- Clothespins to hang orders on the wire
- Card tables and chairs
- Silverware folded in paper napkins
- Salt- and peppershakers for each table
- Homemade menu and tent cards listing specials
- Local newspapers folded and left on a few chairs
- "Men/Women" sign on the bathroom door

MUSIC

Add to the ambiance by selecting an oldies radio station. We like the forties station. Even the drone of the announcer's voice is reminiscent of the nostalgia you're trying to create. If you have a vintage radio (even if it doesn't work), set it out as a prop.

ENTERTAINMENT

Gosh, we don't know, but we think turning your kitchen into a short-order diner should be pretty entertaining in itself. You'll move with balletlike synchronization to keep that coffee brewing, those flapjacks flipping, and those sausages sizzling. And then you'll be able to sit down and enjoy your breakfast as you watch the second shift bob and weave.

> When we hosted the Blue Plate Special, we discovered that our guests enjoyed preparing and serving as much as they did eating. They were prepared for something fun and unusual because we told them to bring their senses of humor and appetites.

Shangri-La-De-Da (de da)

We Americans are geographically challenged. When someone says *island*, we naturally think of the Hawaiian or Caribbean islands. We wanted a more exotic locale for this island party, but after poring over maps and atlases, we decided, heck, we may as well come up with our own.

Welcome to Shangri-La-De-Da (de da). Shangri-la-de-da (de da) is rich in custom. One custom literally brings the whole darn village together. It seems that the Shangi-la-de-da (de da) natives have long honored the island gods with a concoction most delectable: the Sacred Punch. The natives are invited to offer firewater to the Sacerd Punch Bowl. In a magical metamorphosis, the firewater then turns into nectar of the gods.

There's pleasure a-plenty in Shangri-La-De-Da (de da), as we pay homage to the tropical island drink, enjoy age-old island games, and dine on cuisine that goes beyond the usual pupu platter. *Play all night with drink of rum, not to worry when monsoon come!*

INVITATION

By Phone

"Hello, Jan? *Boom boom*. Island drum say *boom boom*. Drink and food to be found—*boom*—beyond next mountain in Shangri-La-De-Da (de da)—*boom*—at seven tonight. As gift to gods, bring firewater—*boom boom*. No gift too small—*boom boom*."

By E-Mail

On the island of Shangri-La-De-Da (de da), the ending of a fine day is saluted as fish leap at the sunset.

Join us in raising our glasses to that moment when the Sun God passes the torch to the Moon Goddess.

The gods will accept gifts in the form of firewater.

Contact Tribal Chief Jim.

MENU

You're likely to find the following menu items on Shangri-La-De-Da (de da). Actually, you could find them on all tropical islands, by virtue of the fact that most islands are located smack-dab in the middle of the sea and on latitudes that are warm and sunny. Use colorful plastic or paper tableware and brightly colored napkins.

Food

- Pan-fried fish sandwiches: Use a blackening seasoning on swordfish, tuna, or salmon. Pan-fry in a combination of butter and Pam. Serve on Cuban or Mexican bread. (If this is not readily available in your area, French bread will do, but it's not as soft.) Garnish with a squeeze of lime, tartar sauce, thinly sliced red onion, tomato, and lettuce.
- Cubed peeled papaya: Add a few shakes of Tabasco and a few squeezes of lime over the cubes. Have cocktail toothpicks available for self-serving.
- Cheese wedges
- Water crackers
- Flavored cream cheeses
- Toasted flatbread rounds
- Sliced apples splashed with lime juice
- Peeled baby carrots in cold water, served in short tumblers
- Mock crab or lobster salad: Serve on seeded, dried slices of cucumbers. Top with a dollop of fish roe.

Beverages

Tropical drinks—the long-held secrets of Shangri-La-De-Da (de da)—are a large part of this party. Colorful plasticware is perfect, and make sure you serve the drinks in big glasses. A tropical drink served in a little glass is like a wool sweater that's been washed in hot water: It's not that it's small, it's just that you *know* it's supposed to be bigger. Also, since this party focuses heavily on libations, it's up to you to make sure your guests are "seaworthy" before they leave.

- Here are some out-of-the-ordinary recipes that will quickly become island favorites:
    - Coquito: In a blender, mix 2 cans coconut cream, 1 can condensed milk, 1 can evaporated milk, 4 egg yolks (optional), ½ cup cognac, 1 teaspoon vanilla extract, 1 quart white rum, and 1 tablespoon ground cinnamon. Serve cold from a pitcher or bowl.
    - *Chichaito*: No matter what we said about big glasses, serve this in a wineglass. It's potentially as potent as a dormant volcano. Combine 1 part anisette, 1 part rum, and a squeeze of lemon juice.
    - Dark and Stormy: Yikes, stripes! Sip slowly—it sounds deadly! Combine 2 ounces dark rum and 2 ounces ginger beer.
    - Whiskey and *Parcha*: Nothing says *tropical* like passion fruit! Mix together 6 ounces parcha juice, 1 ounce Scotch, and lime and lemon juice to taste.
    - Frozen Parcha Cream: Bring on the blender! Combine 4 ounces parcha juice, 2 scoops vanilla ice cream, ⅓ cup cold milk, and 1 ounce gin or vodka.
    - Big-Assed Mama: We made up this recipe ourselves, and it's quite good, if we do say so. In a blender, mix 1 frozen banana, lots of rum (white or dark—it matters not), ice, and 1 cup fresh orange juice till it's the consistency of a shake. Squeeze lime juice on top. Garnish with lime wedge.
- You can also make the usual blender favorites:
    - Piña coladas
    - Margaritas
    - Frozen daiquiris
    - Bahama Mamas

- Don't forget about the Sacred Punch. Dump the firewater contributions into the Sacred Punch Bowl, where your choice of fruit juices, something effervescent (sparkling water, lemon-lime soda, or ginger ale), and citrus slices already await. You'll want to end up with three parts mix to one part liquor. Tropical punches can handle just about any liquor you pour into them, since the other ingredients are so delicious.

PROPS AND DÉCOR

- Tiki torches
- Open fire pit
- Bowls of floating blossoms or floating candles
- Candles if you hold the party indoors

MUSIC

You can play whatever you want. Reggae? Jimmy Buffett? The soundtrack from *South Pacific?* Or are you looking for something a little different? We're going to take this opportunity to talk up a collection of music that we found to be terrific. The Putumayo World Music collection celebrates music from different lands. To order, call their toll-free number at 888-788-8629 or visit their web site at www.putumayo.com. For Shangri-La-De-Da (de da), all of these selections will work:

- *Africa*
- *Caribe! Caribe!*
- *Cuba*
- *A Mediterranean Odyssey: Athens to Andalucia*
- *Reggae Around the World*
- *Afro~Latino*
- *Mambo Yo Yo* by Ricardo Lemvo and Makina Loca
- *A Putumayo Blend: Music from the Coffee Lands*
- *Caribbean Party*
- *Islands*
- *One World*
- *Best of World Music: World Dance Party*

ENTERTAINMENT

There are many traditions on Shangri-La-De-Da (de da). Try these out on your island guests:

- Bamboo Performance Stick Dancing: Four people sit and hold two long bamboo poles (two people at each end) a few inches off the ground. The pairs clap the sticks together to a rhythm, while the other guests take turns dancing between the sticks, trying to keep their ankles from being clapped.

- Sacrifice the Virgins: This is a bit like a mosh pit stage dive. Gather all your strong, strapping men at the bottom of a stepladder. The beautiful "virgins," one by one, throw themselves to the mercy of the men. Do this at your own risk.

- Limbo: In case that stick dancing thing listed above doesn't work out, go with this old favorite.

- Cave Drawings: Create an anthropological history of Shangri-La-De-Da (de da). Fasten a bed sheet to a wall and provide markers. Have guests illustrate the history of the island and its local customs in the form of cave drawings—the nature of which we leave to their imaginations.

> We thought about attire for this party, and here's what we decided. The ladies would be quite lovely in summery sundresses or in something with a tropical print. This might sound gamy as all get-out, but we can't help but see the men in makeshift loincloths (two kitchen towels fastened on the sides with giant safety pins). Those pasty thighs would be exposed all the way up. It might make the island gods angry, but it would provide all kinds of entertainment for the rest of us.

Bakery Dinner

We think fat has gotten a bad rap in the past few decades. To make absolutely certain we knew what we're talking about here, we looked up the word *fat* in several references. One definition of *fat* clearly states, "The best or richest part of anything."

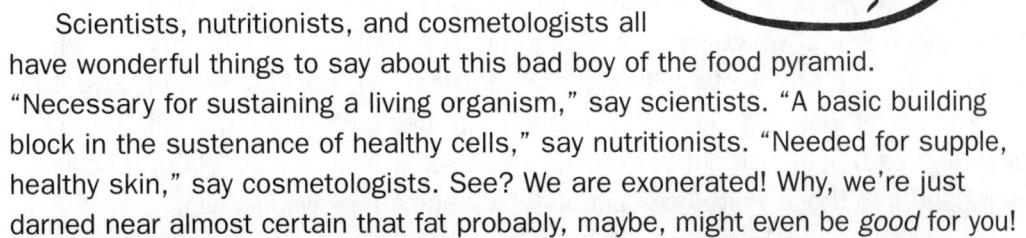

Scientists, nutritionists, and cosmetologists all have wonderful things to say about this bad boy of the food pyramid. "Necessary for sustaining a living organism," say scientists. "A basic building block in the sustenance of healthy cells," say nutritionists. "Needed for supple, healthy skin," say cosmetologists. See? We are exonerated! Why, we're just darned near almost certain that fat probably, maybe, might even be *good* for you!

So let us now pay homage to the "best and richest part" of that food pyramid. We will help you make an entire dinner out of baked goods. To those of you who ask "Why?" we offer the basic Sir Edmund Hilary response, which we guess would have been something like "Why not?" or "Because it's there."

Besides, who among us wants to be tormented in her golden years by the knowledge that she could have made a complete meal out of baked goods, but never realized it until it was too late and until the ol' gallbladder simply wouldn't allow it? Who wants to live with *that* forever and ever?

And so, if only for a night, make friends with fat. Dance with the devil, won't you? You needn't go to the prom with him, but a quick fox trot couldn't hurt.

INVITATION

By Phone

"Whatever you're doing, drop it, because *no way* is it better than what I've got for you here. Come over at seven!"

By E-Mail

Patty cake, patty cake, hungry, man?
Come to my house as fast as you can!
There are doughnuts and beignets and white wine, too,
sitting here waiting for me and for you!

Call Babs!

MENU

If you're looking to legitimize this high-fat affair, calling it an afternoon tea won't even raise an eyebrow. Nor will calling it a bakery brunch. You can, of course, serve this menu at whatever time of day you like. We just call it Bakery Dinner because we can't think of anything more decadent. We would absolutely love it if you served the baked goods still in those white bags. Place them on the table and let guests peek and choose. There's just something exciting about reaching your hand into those white bags and grabbing something wonderful.

Food

- Chocolate éclairs with custard filling
- Cream puffs with real whipped cream
- Almond horns
- Elephant ears
- Apple fritters
- Long johns
- Jelly-filled Bismarcks
- Louisiana crunch cakes
- Dunkin' Donuts Munchkins
- Beignets
- Navajo fry bread or *sopapillas* with honey
- Butter pound cake with lemon glaze
- Meat pies: Those of you who refuse sugar as your main entrée will love these meat pies from the Chinese or Caribbean bakery, if you're lucky enough to

have one nearby. Serve with dipping sauces, such as jalapeño jelly or chutney. You can make homemade meat pies by filling Pillsbury Crescent Rolls with browned ground beef or spicy sausage (like chorizo). Add raisins, tomato sauce, cumin, and cinnamon. Wrap the ingredients in the dough and bake according to the instructions.

Beverages

- Dry white wine, Chardonnay, or French table wine
- Coffee
- Oolong tea
- Cold beer with the meat pies

PROPS AND DÉCOR

Décor? *You don't need no stinking décor! Just eat!*

MUSIC

Go with something that will slide down as easily as the pastries. A few suggestions include anything by:

- Eric Clapton
- Don Henley
- Ry Cooder
- Savage Garden

ENTERTAINMENT

Nothing can match what comes out of those white bags. However, since this gathering is all about food—the good, the bad, and the ugly of it—once you finish licking your chocolate-cream-covered fingers, you may want to throw out this topic for discussion: *(gasp!)* food.

- How about coming up with some family food stories—like the grandma who kept sticking her finger in the cake batter and licking it, the cousin who ate ketchup sandwiches, or even our very own Catholic schoolgirl who went to great lengths for Little Debbies? One of us (who shall remain nameless) used to raid the cache of Little Debbies stored in her parents' deep freezer. Her ingenuity was unmatched because she actually invented the first microwave of sorts: She placed the individually wrapped Little Debbies in the dryer to thaw. After a few minutes in the "high heat/cotton" cycle, the Little Debbies were all gooey and warm, fresh from the dryer.

- Or how about foods you just don't get? Don't you wonder how people can eat something that smells worse than evil itself? (Bleu cheese and durian—the smelliest fruit on earth—come to mind.) Or how about that stuff that is innocuously known as *sweetbread?* One taste and they're not fooling anyone! And how about this little delicacy: sheep's intestines with "natural stuffing"? Now *there's* a conversation topic for dinner! (One of our husbands actually ate this dish. His wife—a woman of great intelligence, breathtaking beauty, and perfection—wouldn't kiss him for weeks.)

> May we leave you with one final thought? We'd like to honor a person who never received the acclaim that he or she so clearly deserves. This person will never win a Nobel Prize and will never go down in the annals of history. This person contributed so much yet received so little recognition in return. In fact, we don't even know his or her name. A moment of silence, please, for the person who invented icing.

Ragin' Cajun

Not long ago, it seemed we were in the mood for Cajun food all the time. Everything that touched our lips had to be spiced with cayenne pepper, and we wanted it hotter than hell's hinges. One night we even made Cajun popcorn for some friends. We'll share here the lesson we learned and the party it prompted.

We discovered that the number one rule when cooking with cayenne pepper is that the pepper has to stick to something. If not, it becomes airborne. The popcorn did not have enough oil for the pepper to stick to, and once that bowl was carried into the room, we lapsed into coughing fits of biblical proportions. After the second handful, we all stopped eating—except one guest. He was not about to be outfoxed by a bowl of popcorn. The munch-and-cough cycle continued until the bowl was empty.

We felt bad about causing someone to cough nearly to the point of a Code Blue. To make it up to him, we created the Ragin' Cajun party and put him at the top of the guest list. This party feeds all the senses and conjures a little voodoo, a lot of spice, and a steamy night in the Big Easy. And all the cayenne pepper you'll see listed here is designed to stay on the food.

INVITATION

By Phone

"Hello, *cher.* Boudreaux and I are offerin' up some o' dat Nawlins hospitality, us. Can y'all be here tonight for dinner at eight, beb?"

By E-Mail

Who do dat voodoo dat you do so well? Well, I do, beb!

Cajun cuisine served up tonight at 8:00 on Bayou [Your Name]. Y'all call.

Laissez les bons temps rouler!

MENU

This party is about flavor. If you have a restaurant, deli, or catering sevice that can put together Cajun dishes, you're in luck. But it's not a big deal if you do the cooking yourself. Cajun food comes together quickly and easily. Make sure your recipes feature the traditional Cajun flavors: celery seed, onion, garlic, cayenne pepper, black pepper, and salt. For the uninitiated Cajun cook, packaged seasonings offer authentic flavor and are available at most grocery stores. Try Zatarain's or Tony Chachere's flavorings. And have plenty of hot sauces on hand, such as Louisiana Gold or Tabasco. (Don't forget to wash your hands after handling spices. If you've ever cooked Cajun and then rubbed your eyes, you won't ever have to be reminded again!) Serve your meal at the table and use earthenware. The smells are fantastic and the colors will add to your "tablescape." Your nice table linens would work great, but don't use anything too fancy. Or how about butcher paper and paper napkins? 'Cause guess what: Dat works, too, *cher!*

Food

The entrées and rice dishes can be served separately or layered into one main "smothered" entrée. All these flavors work well together:

- Jambalaya
- Dirty rice (red beans and rice)
- Green salad with red onions and oil and vinegar dressing
- Snap peas with lime juice, honey, and basil
- Crusty French bread
- Hot pepper cheese corn bread: If you really want to wow your guests, have that corn bread baking just prior to serving. Here's a quick and easy recipe: Pour ⅛ cup corn oil into an 8-inch iron skillet and preheat it to 400°F. Add ¼ pound shredded hot pepper cheese and 2 6-ounce boxes of corn bread batter. Bake 25–35 minutes or until it passes the toothpick test. Invert skillet and shake corn bread onto a plate. Cut into 4 large or 8 skinny pieces.
- Bread pudding or praline sauce served over French vanilla ice cream
- Rice and fruit pudding

Beverages

- Beer: Dixie and Blackened Voodoo beers are both brewed in Louisiana, if you want to be really authentic.
- Red or white wine
- Chilled asti spumante: We like the idea of serving something fancy with a down-home meal.
- Hot or iced coffee after the meal

PROPS AND DÉCOR

Down-home elegance. Paradoxical as that may sound, it's exactly how this party feels to us. It's exotic. It's sensual. But it's down-home comfortable. And you're not going to believe how easy it is. *Big* easy!

- Create the feel of a New Orleans courtyard or a bayou eatery. If outside, wind white icicle lights around the trees, string them in the bushes, and hang them on the fence. If indoors, fasten them to houseplants, fasten them to the top of a window frame, and string them across the ceiling.
- Buy Spanish moss at a floral shop or craft store, pull it apart loosely, and drape it in the trees.
- Votive candles set in Mason jars or old-fashioned glasses half-filled with sand will add to the feel of casual elegance.

MUSIC

Cajun and zydeco or Nawlins jazz? The choice is yours, because there's just no way you can go wrong with one or all of them.

- Cajun and zydeco artists include the following:
  - Beausoleil
  - Steve Riley and the Mamou Playboys
  - Zachary Richard
  - Chubby Carrier and the Bayou Swamp Band
  - Buckwheat Zydeco

- New Orleans jazz artists include the following:
    - Pete Fountain
    - Al Hirt
    - Louis Armstrong
    - The Neville Brothers

ENTERTAINMENT

You know what we'd love? We'd love it if you were to take your time with the meal. *Dine* instead of *eat*. Linger over coffee, crack open more wine or asti, and let the music take you to a place where things are not always what they appear to be.

> There's always another layer of reality at play in New Orleans, don't you think? Tonight, embrace the mystique. Maybe it's the music. Maybe it's the candlelight. Or maybe it's dat voodoo!

Cookbook Pass-Around

Youth and beauty are no match for old age and trickery. We ourselves become more fiendishly clever—"yet retain that dewy sparkle of youth and beauty," add our husbands—the older we get. Listen to this: We came up with a party that virtually guarantees we'll be invited to a friend's dinner party within one month and to other friends' dinner parties every month thereafter.

The Cookbook Pass-Around is not just a party but a *series* of parties that members of your group will host as you pass a cookbook from one friend to the next. The focus is food, and we personally are always delighted to see a little rivalry when it comes to food. We love it when a host tries to outdo last month's host, because it always means good eating.

Get this party going in your group, and you won't regret it. It guarantees a great meal among friends once a month (without you always being the host)!

Note: Because party details differ from cookbook to cookbook, we're going to use the party we hosted for our own friends as an example. To authenticate our menu, we chose a theme. We decided on a Thai barbecue in a beach shack in Phuket, Thailand. When your cookbook gets passed around, every host will have carte blanche. Theme or no theme, this party is a great way to explore interesting menus.

INVITATION

By Phone

"Mike, can you join us for a novel dining experience tonight at seven?" It's always a good idea to pique his interest before you spring that this is a round robin thing.

By E-Mail

Join us tonight at 7:00 for a novel dining experience. Tonight will be the start of something tasty!

Call Bruce for details.

MENU

Our menu was from *The Art of Grilling* by Kelly McCune (Harper & Row, 1990). This cookbook provided simple menus with plenty of flavor. (We never look for sainthood by making things difficult for ourselves.) When you choose your menu, choose foods you enjoy and you can actually cook without becoming crabby. In our circle, we passed around three cookbooks to vary our menus and make dining intriguing. Besides *The Art of Grilling,* we passed around *Sundays at Moosewood Restaurant* by the Moosewood Collective (Fireside, 1990), which showcases a vegetarian bill-of-fare; and *Caribbean Light* by Donna Shields (Doubleday, 1998), which features fabulous island cooking. After dining with our circle of friends for a number of years, we've become familiar with one another's tastes, and we chose our cookbooks accordingly.

Food

Here's what we fixed:

- Thai barbecued chicken
- Snow peas with toasted sesame dressing
- Silver noodles with cucumber, carrots, and rice vinegar
- Lemon ice for dessert (which wasn't included in the cookbook's menu but we added anyway)

Beverages

If your cookbook doesn't suggest beverages, try to pick something that complements the flavor of the food. We thought these beverages would work well with our Thai barbecue:

- Singha, a Thai beer
- Iced tea

PROPS AND DÉCOR

Like food, hosts come in all flavors. Some of you may choose to do a barbecue in Borneo and others may choose to be exactly who you are, where you are. Here are a few props we used to create that casual yet blatantly sensual feel of a Phuket beach shack. We hope they will give you the general idea of how simple it can be to add atmosphere.

- We held the party outdoors on a steamy summer night.
- We covered our table with white butcher paper and used paper towels instead of napkins.
- We used colorful, heavy paper plates and straw-woven place mats.
- Under the table we laid some inexpensive woven beach mats.
- We surrounded the table with houseplants.
- On the table, we set out condiments, such as salt, black pepper, and red pepper flakes.
- We surrounded the party area with tiki torches.
- We hung white Italian lights overhead.

MUSIC

Select music that matches the mood and atmosphere of your dinner. If you have a theme, you might want the music to tie in accordingly. Since Phuket plays host to tourists from all over the world, you'd hear just about anything at a beach shack. Our selections ran the gamut from sultry jazz to Italian crooners to American music from the forties. We sort of winged it, but the result was impressive.

ENTERTAINMENT

- Display your cookbooks before dinner. Our guests salivated at the sumptuous photos of food in our cookbooks. "Oh, I'd love to try this!" someone would squeal. "Oh, you *can!*" we would sing.
- During dinner, explain how the Cookbook Pass-Around works and decide who will host the next party. At our party, cheeks flushed, breaths were held, and hearts pounded as we chose the next host. The lucky winner was Kate, who walked off with all three cookbooks. We couldn't wait for next month!

- And where will you go next? South of the border, down Mexico way? Paris in springtime? To help the next host brainstorm for ideas, consider the potential menus and the props each person might contribute. Also consider when you'll have the next party. You may want to schedule it for a birthday or other special occasion, when an eclectic mix of food is just the ticket. Have a calendar ready and pencil in a date.

> We enjoy giving parties, but we also like going to them. There never seem to be enough dinner party invitations in a season, and Lord knows, it's bad form to beg someone into giving a party. But now that you've read about the Cookbook Pass-Around, we hope you realize there's more than one way to skin a cat.

Divide and Conquer

May we speak freely? We don't know about you, but we've never had much luck at a potluck.

We don't want to offend, but why do members of a church (or synagogue or temple) have such a fervent desire to make Jell-O? Because sure as the sun rises in the east, there's more Jell-O at a church potluck than there was manna during those forty years in the desert. And we're betting no one's nearly as excited about Jell-O as Moses was about manna.

Don't pretend you haven't seen this. For the spring potluck, someone always shows up with a Jell-O bunny mold surrounded by—*oh, the wonder of it all!*—green coconut. Within an hour, the black jellybean eyes have bled into the Jell-O, and the bunny looks as if it came straight out of *Children of the Corn*. Standing nearby without fail is its creator, needling people into "just a little taste of the ear."

When reduced to the simplest form, the Divide and Conquer party is a potluck with one important exception: *You* will take on the title of Supreme Potluck Commander in order to make it an elegant affair. And if anybody asks, "Should I bring Jell-O?" the answer is no.

INVITATION

By Phone

"Hi, Cindy, it's Tim. Are you free for dinner at eight? We're hosting an oxymoron tonight: an elegant potluck. By all means, dress for the occasion. Here's what I want you to bring…"

By E-Mail

Come for dinner and witness an oxymoron! We're inviting you to an elegant potluck. Call before 4:00 to discuss what you'll bring.

Dinner's at 8:00.

MENU

As Supreme Potluck Commander, you'll contribute the main dish. Ask each guest to provide one or more items to complete your menu. The key is to create something elegant without demanding too much on short notice. (Then again, making a chicken breast is no more demanding than making a hot dog, when it comes right down to it.) When setting a table, most of us use either fine holiday linens and china or paper napkins and plates. But here's a chance to use that in-between stuff. Mix and match complementary styles and colors if you don't have enough of any one set.

Food

- Here's what you can prepare for the main entrée:
  - Chicken breasts, pork chops, pork tenderloin: Season or marinate the meat as early as possible, then toss it on the grill. (We live in Illinois, and we grill year 'round, so excuses about weather are not acceptable.) If you don't have access to a grill, the broiler is the next best thing for that flame-broiled taste and texture.
- Have your guests bring the following dishes:
  - Salad: If your guest wants to get creative, suggest he make a tossed salad with bite-size pieces of greens, veggies, fruit, cheese, seeds, and nuts. Or how about a Greek salad with tomato, cucumber, onion, black pepper, olive oil, and rice vinegar? Spinach salad with bacon dressing? Ask the guest to keep the dressing on the side and covered, especially if it's strong, such as bleu cheese. (*FYI:* When one of us doesn't like a particular food, she *has* to have it "on the side and covered." It's such a big issue, she insisted we put it in the book.)
  - Bread: Is your guest strapped for time? Believe it or not, convenience stores can sell wonderful French bread. The secret is warming it for five minutes in a preheated oven. Frozen French rolls or bread can be popped into a hot oven, too. Your guest can even bake up the crescent rolls that come from the cardboard tube you *thwack!* open against the counter. Can your guest make corn bread? Have her top the batter with a few roasted red peppers. The peppers will bake into the mix and look groovy.

- Veggies: Your guest will likely have the frozen variety on hand. If he has fresh asparagus, fate has surely smiled upon you. Have him steam the spears in the microwave by standing them in a half-inch of water. If not, have your guest bring corn, broccoli, or mixed veggies. Sprinkle them with hot sauce or lime or lemon juice.
- Rice, pasta, or couscous: If your guest wants to make it special, have her use stock instead of water for extra flavor. She can also add some herbs and a little olive oil.
- Dessert: Does a guest have bananas? Have him pop sliced bananas, brown sugar, butter, and rum in the microwave to make a great Bananas Foster topping for vanilla ice cream (which another guest can provide). Served in stemware, even plain old ice cream becomes *très élégant*. If your guest can bring brownies, dress them up by dusting the serving plates with a bit of cocoa or confectioners' sugar. Fruit makes a great dessert if your guest is pinched for time. Strawberries and green grapes are perfect anytime.

Beverages

- As Supreme Potluck Commander, you can call upon the troops to help with beverages, too. Appoint guests to bring the following:
  - Wine: A bottle of red, a bottle of white. Like the "no white shoes before Memorial Day" rule, wine rules no longer exist. Tell your guest what you're making for the main dish, but then let her choose the wine.
  - Beer: Your guest can bring beer for the meal, but ask him to get something a little special. We are not snobs, no, we surely are not, but dark ale served in a tall pilsner will look nicer on your table than Bud in a bottle.
- Yes, you're Supreme Potluck Commander, but you should also be a good host. Have the following beverages available for your guests:
  - Pitchers or carafes of ice water on the table
  - Coffee with or after dessert: Ready the coffeemaker in advance so all you have to do is flick the switch to let your guests know that something good is a-comin'. Unlike coffee served at other potlucks, this cuppa joe will actually be (*gasp*) dark brown instead of light tan, and it won't come from an eighty-cup metal urn either!

PROPS AND DÉCOR

- Pull out the candles. (Yes, we do use candles a lot!) How about creating a path of votive candles in Mason jars along your sidewalk or even along the driveway? Make the evening feel special for your guests before they even get into the house. Inside, place a small votive candle on a saucer or in a coffee mug at each place setting.
- If you have houseplants, surround the table with them.

MUSIC

Go with soft dinner music. Try light jazz or mellow melodies by the following artists:

- Diana Krall
- Ella Fitzgerald
- Herb Alpert
- Laura Fygi
- Sergio Mendes and Brasil '66
- Johnny Mercer

ENTERTAINMENT

At dinner, enjoy your handiwork as Supreme Potluck Commander and enjoy conversation with your friends. When clearing the table, put on a dance tune, and all at once it's dinner and dancing. Over coffee and dessert, feel free to put on well-known sing-along music, and if the spirit moves any of your guests to sing, by all means, let them have at it.

This party needn't go longer than two hours, and we imagine everyone out of there no later than ten o'clock. If we want to "do this more often," then we shouldn't make it a big deal in the first place. Anyone who's been married longer than five years will recognize this logic. When the guy's winkin' and blinkin' and lookin' for nookie, he often pulls out this old argument: "Well, maybe if this happened more often, it wouldn't seem like such a big deal." Uh.... while we *do* promote the heck out of that concept when it comes to partying, we decline comment when it comes to nookie.

Chinatown

We won't make you do anything nearly as complicated or confusing as Faye Dunaway and Jack Nicholson did in *Chinatown,* the movie. Chinatown, the party, is much simpler, and it all started when we thought about the typical Chinese takeout meal. "Let's get Chinese takeout!" is invariably a wonderful and tasty idea (especially if you're supposed to cook that night), but your table usually ends up looking like the desktop of an overworked private eye of questionable hygiene and dubious income (what with all those greasy little white cartons lying around). It is our humble opinion that we can do better.

We figured out a way to beautifully combine the goodness of your own cooking with the ease of Chinese takeout. We whipped up one sweet-and-sassy (bet you thought we were going to say sweet-and-sour!) little dinner party. Yes, this is yet another sneaky way to make it look as if you did an awful lot of work, thereby opening yourself to great accolades and admiration. Taking our cue from *Chinatown,* the movie, where lies ran rampant, we reasoned, "Why should the party version be any different?" Go ahead and pretend you did all the cooking. Your guests may believe you. Or not.

INVITATION

By Phone

"Mary Jane, Confucius says you have a hearty appetite. How about helping Mac and I bring Chinatown to our house tonight? Can you and Bob be here at seven?"

By E-Mail

Confucius says honorable Mary Jane and Bob are invited to join Diane and Mac tonight at 7:00 for Chinese feast. Call Diane before 5:00.

MENU

Such a tasty feast deserves special presentation. Place silverware rolled in a napkin horizontally across each plate. On top of this, place a set of chopsticks diagonally.

Food

- Sesame flank steak with green onions and almonds: Just marinate that steak in Worcestershire sauce, garlic, and ground pepper, then grill or broil it. Toast sesame seeds in a dry pan. Sprinkle over the steak prior to serving. Slice the steak thinly along the grain, add salt and pepper, and serve it over white rice cooked in water flavored with five-spice powder. Garnish the meat and rice with finely snipped green onions, slivered almonds, and the sesame seeds.
- Asian vegetables: Find these ready-to-cook in the frozen food section. Microwave them without adding water until they're al dente. Toss with Mongolian Fire Oil and garnish with slivered almonds.
- Side dishes: Get as many sides from a Chinese takeout restaurant as your heart desires. From moo goo gai pan to duck's feet, have at it. Serve the food from your own pretty dishes. We won't tell a soul. (If you want to be really sneaky, add your own garnishes. For example, add cashews to the sweet-and-sour pork or snip some fresh basil leaves over that basil fried rice.)
- Almond cookies and ginger ice cream for dessert: We love making our own ginger ice cream. Stir freshly ground or powdered ginger into softened vanilla ice cream then refreeze.

Beverages

- Asian beer: A few of the more readily available brands include Tsingtao and Red Dragon (Chinese) and Sapporo and Kirin (Japanese).
- Warm sake: Yes, we know it's not Chinese, but it will work with your menu nonetheless. Remember, use small glasses. Trust us.
- Tea: Brew a pot of your favorite or place a small basket on the table filled with a variety of individually wrapped tea bags. Try oolong, Earl Gray, jasmine, or peach tea.

PROPS AND DÉCOR

- *Oshiboris:* Okay, again, it's Japanese, but it's a marvelous idea. Before guests arrive, roll washcloths and arrange them in a pyramid on a platter. Pour some water over the washcloths, then pop the platter into the microwave till you can see steam. Just before serving dinner, use short tongs to offer washcloths to guests so they can wipe their hands. As soon as you have given out the last towel, start your way back around the table again to retrieve the used cloths. Nobody wants to sit there holding a wet cloth, which will become a *cold* wet cloth in less than sixty seconds.
- Grass place mats or runner
- Lantern luminaries: These are inexpensive, and you can usually find them at a party store. Placed on the floor, they will create ambient lighting from below, which will make interesting shadows on the ceiling. Safety first, though, so keep them out of walkways.
- Pillar candles on small saucers set on the table: Use unscented candles of varying heights for added interest.
- Water garden: If you have time and feel creative, here's an idea that would make a lovely "tablescape." Half-fill a wide, shallow bowl, such as a pasta bowl, with water. Float petals and candles on the water. You can stop there if you like, or if you want to get more Zenlike, add small, decorative rocks. But remember: Less is more.

MUSIC

Soothing Asian music you might hear when you're getting a massage will work nicely for this party. Actually, any soothing (as opposed to energetic or raucous) music will be absolutely fine.

ENTERTAINMENT

You really won't need to do anything elaborate. Just enjoy the meal (since you *slaved away* at that stove all day!). But if the spirit moves you, here's another idea: Include a pen and note pad at each place setting. (That in itself should get people talking. "Ooh, what is *this* fanciness, now?") Guests are invited to write "fortunes" that will be placed in a bowl and randomly drawn by other guests during tea and dessert. And if someone happens to have a fortune in mind for a specific guest, he or she is welcome to designate the fortune to a recipient. And let's just see if eyes don't flash when that recipient reads it.

If you're really pressed for time, don't bother cooking that sesame flank steak or Asian vegetable medley. Order it all from a takeout restaurant, but be sure to take the time to add your own garnishes. Here's an easy way to remember this important step, courtesy of the climactic Dunaway-Nicholson scene in the movie that bears the same name as this party:

"The almonds go on the steak!" *(Slap!)*

"The almonds go on the vegetables!" *(Slap!)*

"They go on the steak!" *(Slap!)*

"They go on the vegetables!" *(Slap!)*

"The steak!" *(Slap!)*

"The vegetables! *(Slap!)*

"They go on the steak *and* the vegetables!"

Odd but Amusing

Wild Abandon

We know what you envisioned when you read the title "Wild Abandon." You imagined someone spinning out of control, a whirling dervish, one quite mad with wine—maybe even *naked!* Are we right?

Well, we admit we gave our imaginations a little more rope than normal when we concocted this party. But first things first: The action takes place in bathing suits. (Let's face it: At the department meeting the next morning, you won't want to remember what someone's fanny or giblets or what-have-you looked like.) This party may be wild, but it doesn't take you all the way into the snake pit.

This party is perfect for a summer night when it's so hot and so humid, one may take leave of his senses and feel like a cat on a hot tin roof. Under the influence of oppressive heat, you'll want to cut loose and shrug off inhibitions as well as (some) clothing.

Dare we use the word *foreplay?* If we can, we'd like to draw a parallel: Like endless foreplay, this party is titillating, and that's about it. It doesn't go beyond that. When it boils right down, this party's actually good, clean fun that only feels a little naughty. You will judge how far you'll venture into the realm of wildness. We realize the line in the sand is drawn somewhere different for everyone. But by all means, go right up to that line and maybe even put your toe over it.

INVITATION

By Phone

"Dahling, it's so hot! Big Daddy and I wanna know if y'all are feeling as crazy in this heat as we are! 'Cause if you are, how 'bout comin' over and bein' crazy with us?"

By E-Mail

It's so hot...let's get crazy! Experience it tonight in Bali Hai, Neverland, and a Tennessee Williams play all rolled into one. You're not gonna wanna miss this!

Call before I change my mind! The heat, you know, can make one quite mad.

MENU

Your menu items may not necessarily go well together. Just serve whatever you consider decadent. The higher the fat content, the happier you'll be. Set it all out as a buffet and let the guests indulge whenever they wish.

Food

- Häagen Dazs: It'd be the height of all that is unholy to have ice-cream stations set up all over your back yard. Set out insulated buckets or coolers containing quarts of your favorite ice cream and let guests eat right out of the containers. Have spoons nearby.
- Caviar on ice served on a lovely tray
- Liqueur-filled chocolates
- Assorted cheeses and crackers
- Peanut butter: Go ahead. Dip your fingers and eat it right out of the jar. C'mon, ya know ya wannoo!
- Shrimp platter and cocktail sauce
- Cold crab salad

Beverages

- Champagne (Truth be told, we prefer asti spumante) and beer: Keep on ice and set up stations in the back yard or party area.
- World's Largest Margarita: Get a plastic "single baby" kiddie pool. Wet the rim and pour salt onto it. Then pour margarita mix and tequila into the pool till it's at least half full. Get quarter-inch plastic tubing from a hardware store, wash it, and cut it into several pieces. Stick the pieces in the margarita and use them as community "straws." Also, have ladles, glasses, and lime slices nearby.

- World's Largest Martini: Same procedure as the margarita above, but how about a ton of olives floating in the pool? We envision a little olive bobbing.

PROPS AND DÉCOR

- Plant tiki torches throughout the back yard or the party area, but allow for a few dark pockets.
- Hang candles in buckets from the trees. Just make sure you use wire (not flammable twine or anything like that) to secure them far from other branches. No mood on this planet is worth that dry evergreen going up in flames. Then it truly would be a night beyond imagination.
- Provide towels, napkins, and maybe even a change of clothes for someone who crosses a bridge too far.

MUSIC

- You could go with frenzied music, such as the soundtrack from *Zorba the Greek*.
- Or you could go with something a little campy, like the soundtrack from *South Pacific*.
- Or you could go with sultry sounds and "high-fat" content, like stuff by Satchmo, k.d. lang, and Sarah Vaughan.
- Of course, you could always go with a combination of all three types.

ENTERTAINMENT

My, my. Could that actually be the faint scent of *myrrh* in the air? You won't have to orchestrate the entertainment for this party, because if the props are all in place, people will play, get nuts, and have fun.

- Tell your guests to wear their bathing suits under their clothes, because as sure as we're sittin' here, clothes are going to come off. It may be hard to get some of the ladies to display themselves, so have a few large T-shirts on hand for those who balk. With the men, that's usually not a problem. In fact, the challenge will probably be to get them to keep their bathing suits *on*.
- Fill a large kiddie pool with water and bubble bath. Invite as many people to frolic in it as it will hold.

- Fill a large bucket with shaving cream and try your hands at body painting.
- Set out bottles of bubbles and let guests languidly sit around and fill the air with bubbles.
- Lawn sprinklers will allow people to rinse off and get loony at the same time.
- Hang a hose over a tree limb and attach a mister. Cool off in what will feel like a wet cloud, but it won't be enough to rinse off. You'll never get as wet as you want under the mister. (Oh, my—did *we* say that?)
- Shampoo one another's hair.
- Start a Silly String battle.
- In the light cast by tiki torches against the garage or a fence, do some shadow silliness. Here's your chance to do that fan dance you've always wanted to do. Or pull out the veils and fly around insanely like Salome in *The Greatest Story Ever Told*.

Wild Abandon may carry late into the evening. And over the water cooler the next morning, should any of your gypsies, tramps, and thieves be heard to say, "Papa woulda shot him if he knew what he'd done!" you'll know your party was a hedonistic success.

Progressive Leaf Raking

It's autumn. One of those bright, blue, Helen Hunt Jacksonesque September days. You're out raking your yard, and your neighbors are out raking their yards. One of two things will invariably happen.

Scenario Number One: You engage in conversation with your fellow rakers, and everyone starts hollering back and forth loud enough to get the dogs barking. A plane flies overhead, and now no one can hear anything. Hands are cupped behind ears. The word *huh?* reverberates throughout the neighborhood. The cacophony sets your teeth on edge.

Scenario Number Two: You're outside, just doing your job, ma'am. You don't want to be standoffish, so you offer your neighbors a smile here, a nod there, till sooner or later you get tired of politely acknowledging one another's presence. You carry leaf bags to the curb and try to think up something clever to say before you converge with a neighbor who's doing the same. "Boy-oh-boy, the leaves are sure coming down *this* year!"

Put an end to this kind of nonsense once and for all by adapting Tom Sawyer's M.O. for manipulating others, and invite the whole neighborhood to a progressive leaf-raking party. Before you know it, everyone's front yards will be raked, and everyone will have fun accomplishing the task together. Pack up the babies, grab the old ladies—*everyone* goes!

INVITATION

By Phone (or more likely by hollering)

Start singing, "You've to accentuate the positive, eliminate the negative, latch on to the affirmative. C'mon and let me tell ya what I mean!" Once you get their attention, talk up your plan, and we bet they'll take you up on it.

By E-Mail

It's likely that the spirit won't move you to throw this party until you're actually in the throes of raking. But in case you have the foresight to set this up in advance, send out the same song in e-mail form:

"You've got to ac-cen-tu-ate the pos-i-tive,
E-lim-in-ate the neg-a-tive,
Latch on to the af-firm-a-tive.
C'mon and let me tell ya what I mean!"

Call Wilma right now!

MENU

Since this party may be about as instant as it gets, someone might have to make a quick run to the grocery or deli. Use paper- or plasticware. Set up a buffet at your house, or with enough notice, have each participating household host a different part of the meal: Chili at the Smith's, cider at the Jones's, dessert at the Brown's. (When you say it that way, it actually sounds cosmopolitan, like "breakfast in Paris, lunch in Istanbul, dinner in Singapore.")

Food

- Chili: Provide chopped onions, grated Cheddar, sour cream, hot sauce, chili powder, and chopped jalapeños on the side. Keep it simmering in a slow cooker and have ladles available so guests can help themselves. Serve in Styrofoam cups or paper mugs.
- Garlic bread warm from the oven
- Chicken noodle soup for the kidlets: Always a crowd pleaser. (Serve in Styrofoam cups or paper mugs, but make sure it's not too hot.) Provide unseasoned bread or soft breadsticks.
- Corn bread with cayenne pepper
- Taffy apples: It may be worth the advent of winter just to bite into one of these babies. (Have some wet wipes available!)
- Peanut butter, chocolate chip, and oatmeal-raisin cookies
- Maple fudge

Beverages

- Bottled water
- Spiced apple cider: Make it in a slow cooker and keep it simmering.
- Apple juice in boxes for kids
- Hot cocoa
- Flavored "international" coffees

PROPS AND DÉCOR

Besides the obvious—rakes, cotton work gloves, and leaf bags—we couldn't think of anything else that's needed.

MUSIC

Since you'll be outside, get a few participants to pull out their boom boxes. Tune in to a radio station everyone can agree on, and enjoy the polyphony.

ENTERTAINMENT

- While we agree that being near one another and whistling while you work is tough to beat, it doesn't hurt to add a little diversion. Play a few games of "Name That Tune" when the deejay doesn't announce the name of the song in advance.
- You'll no doubt want to keep the kids somewhat entertained, or the adults will get ornery if the little sweeties leap into the just-raked piles.
  - Hand them rakes. (Kids love helping adults. Really, they do!) A word of warning: Kids are completely oblivious to the four feet of rake that sticks out behind them. Stay out of the line of fire. A stick in the fanny leaves no one laughing.
  - Send them to someone's back yard to play under adult supervision. Let them take advantage of the leaves *not* being raked.

> It's best to move the party along and get all the yards raked before people run out of steam. If your tired guests make their way back home and their unraked leaves are still there, don't be surprised if they seek revenge by pulling out that leaf blower at six the next morning.

Hubristic Tour

hu•bris (hyoo´bris) *n.* Extreme arrogance, overweening pride: *Jane was filled with hubris as she encountered a plywood cutout of the ever-popular "fanny in the garden" in her neighbor's yard.* — **hu•bris–tic** (-bris´tik) *adj.* Affected with, marked by, causing, or expressing hubris: *Jane suppresses a hubristic laugh whenever she views ornaments, such as does and fawns or any other life form, in a state of rigor mortis on a homeowner's front lawn.* — **hub•ris´tic•al•ly** *adv.* In a hubristic manner: *Jane invited her friends to tour the neighborhood hubristically in an attempt to poke fun at tasteless lawn ornaments, landscaping, and holiday decorations, and then to return to her house for refreshments and smugness.*

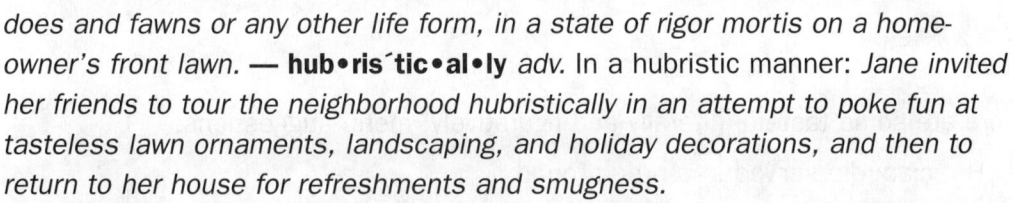

All right, all right! We're guessing a few tongues are clucking over this one. But come on. This party is just another way to inject a little levity into life and to not take it so doggone seriously, for the love of Mike! Besides, we know darned well you've had hubristic thoughts without any prompting from us whatsoever—like the time in the Upper Peninsula when you drove past that house with two pink flamingos planted right there in the permafrost. We know you were thinking this sarcastic little thought, so let us say it out loud for you: "Why, how *natural!* I wonder if those are *real!*"

INVITATION

By Phone

In your best upper-crust accent: "Dickieee! Niles here! What say you and Clarice join us for a bit of a hubristic tour this afternoon? A pompous promenade, if you will. Okay? Ducky!"

By E-Mail

Mother may have told you, "If you don't have anything nice to say, don't say anything at all."

Well, we're gonna say it anyway.

Join us on a hubristic tour this afternoon and plan to stay for posthubristic smugness.

MENU

After the tour, guests will return to your home. (By that time, you'll be convinced it's the last bastion of good taste in your community.) Set up a buffet and use your best linens and tableware.

Food

Here are some tasteful (literally and figuratively) menu suggestions:

- Hot clam dip served in a bread round
- Tomato bisque: For a quick version that tastes great, add sherry and a splash of hot sauce to your favorite tomato soup.
- Caesar salad: Add sliced seasoned chicken breasts to the greens if you really want to be a sport.
- *Salade niçoise*
- Cold, thinly sliced salmon with cucumber-dill sauce (Packaged salmon is available at the grocery store.)
- Caviar or good fish roe

Beverages

Provide everyone with the beverage of his or her choice to maximize the sip-and-snicker factor on the tour. (*Naturally*, if you'll be driving, you know better than to bring anything alcoholic.) Serve whatever feels a little highfalutin. Here are some suggestions:

- Gin and tonics: Always a crowd pleaser, we say.
- Vodka tonics: Especially popular with the horsy set, these are. And tonight, you'll be a member of the horsy set—the high-horsy set, that is.

- Wine
- Champagne
- Mimosas: Just add OJ to that champagne.
- Iced tea
- Lemonade
- Tonic with lime

PROPS AND DÉCOR

If you're going out on foot after dark, have those snooty guests of yours bring flashlights—oh, *excuse* us! We mean, have them bring *torches*, dahling. These are merely for lighting the way, so don't shine them on any objects of ridicule. If streetlights or moonlight can't illuminate a yard, move on.

MUSIC

Either before or after the tour, play anything that makes you feel like a snob. Here are some artists whose music you might want to sample:

- Cole Porter
- Duke Ellington
- Benny Goodman
- Paolo Conte
- Pink Martini
- Cesaria Evora

ENTERTAINMENT

- You'll either hoof it around the neighborhood or drive. Naturally, if you're on foot, you'll want to be discreet about all this nonsense. You'll promenade past two gold bald eagles at the end of a driveway (to create that cozy Fort Bragg feeling, we guess), and you'll gaze upon more gazing globes than there are reasons to gaze into them. You'll want to hoot, scream, and point. But we urge you to wait till you get home. If some overzealous member of your group attempts to place a little note (asking "Why?! Why?!") in a mailbox, he must be stopped!

- There will be no shortage of material if you host this party around Halloween or Christmas. Those two holidays in particular seem to be catalysts for bad displays.

- A variation would be to send out reconnaissance teams. Each team will be equipped with a video camera, digital camera, or instant camera. If you like, choose someone to narrate the video footage, creating something along the lines of a Sundance Film Festival short or a PBS documentary. At a predetermined time, the teams will reconvene, and you'll review the footage in the privacy of your home. The group that captures the best example of lawn ornament debauchery will be declared the winner.

> Lest any of us host this party and then plan to ride off on our absolute highest horse, let us heed the words of T. S. Eliot as he describes what happened to Phlebas the Phoenician from *The Waste Land*. Phlebas was once alive, on top of the world, captain of his own ship. The next thing he knew, the sea "picked his bones in whispers"! And so we are cautioned: "Consider Phlebas, who was once handsome and tall as you." Yes, *you*. The fates could turn. You could develop bad taste. Next thing you know, you could have a plywood fanny in your own front yard.

Munich Meets Milwaukee

Love beer and brats? Looking for a way to justify the consumption of large quantities of both? Then host your very own Oktoberfest.

Throughout the years, we have seen Oktoberfests pop up all over the place. Traditionally held in early autumn, we've seen them held anytime during the season, which begins when the first school bus appears on the horizon around Labor Day and continues right up until the snowflakes begin to fall.

Even more annoying, Oktoberfests have become outlets for vendors selling anything from foot cream to vibrating chairs. We're here to tell you, as ardent as that community social committee might be, there is simply no way to create anything that looks like Munich in a strip mall parking lot. At the very least, at the Oktoberfest you'll host right in your home, you won't be subjected to an "*It slices, dices, and juliennes!*" demonstration next to your keg.

More importantly, your Oktoberfest will be as authentic as you can get in the States, because we're going to show you how to host it in true Wisconsin style. Ah, Wisconsin! Home to many, many German descendants! Just smell that dairy air! California may have its vineyards and its Hollywood, Florida may have its sunshine and its beaches, but Wisconsin has its supper clubs, its Packers, its brats, its beer, plus more Oktoberfests than there are days in October.

INVITATION

By Phone

"Hey, Jen, now's the time to roll out the barrel, 'cause the gang's all here!" That should put Jen directly into the Oktoberfest spirit. Or not. Either way, it's a good opener that suggests what the party is about without sounding too beery.

By E-Mail

Roll out the barrel! We'll have a barrel of fun! Join us tonight at 7:00 for our very own Oktoberfest celebration!

Call Terri before 5:00.

MENU

Attention, gallbladders! There's no shortage of fat in this menu! But it's exactly what you might see at an honest-to-goodness Wisconsin Oktoberfest. Go with colorful paper- or plasticware.

Food

- Brats, brats, and more brats: (For the uninitiated, *brat* is short for *bratwurst* and is pronounced "braht.") If we can sing the praises of any particular brand, let us honor Johnsonville Brats right here and now. Brats are especially tasty when you parboil them in beer and onions then toss them on the grill.
- Buns: We just want to make sure you spring for brat buns. If you pick up regular hot dog buns, you'll have to deal with a few inches of brat sticking out each end of the bun.
- Condiments, such as diced raw onions, horseradish, pickle relish, and a variety of mustards
- Summer sausage, that ubiquitous Wisconsin favorite
- Assortment of crackers
- Cheese!: Cheddar cheese, Swiss cheese, Kaukauna Klub cheese spreads, pepper cheese, salami cheese, cheese curds, cheese logs, cheese popcorn, string cheese, Cojack cheese, mozzarella cheese, Monterey jack cheese, American cheese, bleu cheese, Parmesan cheese, cottage cheese, Edam cheese, Jarlsberg cheese, Gouda cheese, feta cheese, Camembert cheese, Brie cheese, Roquefort cheese, provolone cheese, brick cheese, cheese dip, cheese fondue, cheese soup, cheesecake, cheese and crackers, cheese and fruit...*That's, that's about it.*
- Hot dish: In Wisconsin, Michigan, and Minnesota, *casserole* goes by the name *hot dish,* with the accent on *hot.*

- Salad: If you really want to be authentic, Jell-O—not greens—will be the foundation for your salad. Toss in marshmallows, and you're golden. The three aforementioned states frequently blur the line that separates a salad from a dessert.
- Bars: We could not even begin to touch upon the endless varieties of dessert bars that exist. But do not shortchange your guests of this staple. Within a five-hundred-mile radius of the Great Lakes, bars are expected at any event wherever two or three are gathered, and any church cookbook will attest to that fact.

Beverages

You can go two ways with the beer: You can get a keg, which is what you would likely find at an Oktoberfest. Or you could offer several varieties of bottled or canned beer. Guests can sample small amounts (you can pick up sample-size plastic cups at a party store), or they can choose a different kind every time they're ready for another round. The only caveat is that you need to make certain that the guests are roadworthy before you allow them to leave, since beer does play a starring role.

- Any good liquor store should offer a variety of beer. Many brands also offer a "light" variation. Here are some brands to choose from:
    - Anchor Porter (United States)
    - Ballentine's XXX Ale (United States)
    - Bass & Co's Bale Ale (England)
    - Beck's (Germany)
    - Black Horse (United States)
    - Coors (United States)
    - Corona (Mexico)
    - Grolsch (Holland)
    - Guinness Stout (Ireland)
    - Heineken (Holland)
    - Küppers Kölsch (Germany)
    - Molson (Canada)
    - Red Stripe (Jamaica)
    - Sheaf Stout (Australia)
    - St. Pauli Girl (Germany)
    - Watney's Red Barrel (England)
    - Würzburger (Germany)
- Here are some nonalcoholic beers you may wish to offer as well:
    - Bass Barbican (England)
    - Clausthaler (Germany)
    - Elan Swiss (Switzerland)
    - Kallber (England)

- Kingsbury (United States)
- Metbrau (United States)
- Moussy (Switzerland)
- Saint Michael's (United States)
- Würzburger Nonalcoholic (Germany)

PROPS AND DÉCOR

- If you want to have a Wisconsin Oktoberfest atmosphere, then you'll have to come up with some shining examples of taxidermy, because like German *Bierhausen*, Wisconsin watering holes and supper clubs often display stuffed and static goods from the woods. We'd also accept a nice "lawn deer" (See "Hubristic Tour" on page 127.) And certainly, if even that eludes you, we think it would be funny indeed if you did your best with cardboard and a paper bag. Construct the animal of your choosing and put that sucker on the wall. You could also get creative with plush animals.

- A Wisconsin bar or supper club, like a German *Bierhaus*, has dim incandescent lighting, but it's perfectly appropriate if you take your Oktoberfest outdoors, weather permitting. (In fact, it's more likely you will.)

MUSIC

- Begin with a lively set of polkas as guests arrive. We're guessing most of you don't have these in your collection, but your library will come in handy. Our library has at least one CD that includes yodeling.

- If guests tire of the "Old World," switch to country, which is really popular in Wisconsin. (Every once in a while, though, sneak in a polka, so guests can grab their favorite girls and give them a whirl!)

ENTERTAINMENT

Anything else may pale in the shadow of the beer, brats, and polkas, but you can add these activities for even more excitement:

- "Guess Your Weight" booth: Just bring out your bathroom scale and see if you get any takers.

- Rope the *Fräulein* contests: Here's where the *Herren* lasso the *Damen* with a soft rope.

- Displays of might and brawn: Everyone loves arm-wrestling, tugs of war, and empty keg tosses.
- Carrying contests: Though this is typically done using beer steins, load a tray with plastic or paper cups of water, and see who can get to the finish line with the fewest spills.

> When it comes to authentic "Old World" Oktoberfest costumes, we see a real disparity. Women are outfitted in garb from which Victoria's Secret might have taken a cue, what with the laced-up bodices, plunging décolletages, and all. And with the hiking and woodland-living in Bavaria, we readily admit there may be a necessity for men to wear leather shorts, but do they need to be held up with suspenders? If the suspenders aren't enough to make anyone look like a three-year-old, that added crosspiece makes grown men appear as if they can't keep their suspenders from falling either! To whom, we ask, do those lusty, busty women turn when their men look like Pinocchio?

Whine and Cheese

Sometimes we think we're so darn clever, don't we? Just when we're sure we've outsmarted life, lo and behold, it gives us a swift kick in the pants to show us that *no*, we're not as smart as we imagine.

Like the time we were driving on Highway 10 through rural Wisconsin. Back then, Highway 10 was a two-lane road, although traffic probably warranted four lanes years earlier. Anyway, we had been stuck behind a truck with a horse trailer for about a half-hour. We couldn't pass because of constant oncoming traffic.

Then we came to the small town of Neillsville. Here's our chance, we thought. Why, we'd just go real fast through the back streets, and then get back on Highway 10 before the truck has a chance to make it through town! It's a shocker we didn't get a speeding ticket after we took the turnoff behind the Piggly Wiggly, because we positively hauled rump through the maze of back streets.

At the highway junction at the other end of town, as we waited for an oncoming vehicle to pass before we could whip back on the highway, we smirked smugly, secure in the knowledge that our prowess could outsmart anyone, anywhere. Why, a two-minute dash through Neillsville and we *had* to be ahead of that stupid horse! Imagine the looks on our faces when we discovered that the vehicle we were waiting for was the truck pulling that very horse.

Now, one has two options when ironic things like this happen: laugh or whine away. Our Whine and Cheese party provides a forum for your guests to choose both.

INVITATION

By Phone

"Sheila, tonight we're going to laugh at life's ironies. You have to come and put in your two cents!"

136

By E-Mail

Brothers and Sisters! Life is ironic, so come lay your burden down! Come taste the wine! Come *feeeel* the cheese! Can I get an amen! Have mercy!

Tonight at 7:00, let us laugh at life and its twisted plan for us!

Call Brother Bill before 4:00.

MENU

Let people congregate wherever they seem to gravitate in your home, be it the sitting room, dining room, or kitchen. This is to be a mirth-filled evening of eating and yapping, and it doesn't really matter where the fun takes place. Use your everyday tableware.

Food

- Jalapeño cheese
- Smoked Gouda
- Cheddar aged until it crumbles when you slice it
- Kaukauna Klub and Merkt's spreads (Oh, we love these!)
- Flavored cream cheeses
- Cold, sliced smoked salmon
- Crackers
- Quick, easy hors d'oeuvres, like the oh-so-many things you can make with Triscuits (Recipes on the box!)
- Cashews
- Chocolates (They go beautifully with w[h]ine and cheese.)
- Flavored breadsticks: Place them in a wineglass for a nice presentation.
- Sliced Granny Smith apples: Dip them in peanut butter. Enforce the double-dipping rule as you see fit. If you're like us, the more you like someone or the more attractive he is, the more you'll be apt to let him get away with double dipping.

Beverages

Here are a few types of wines we happen to like, but there are probably equally as many you happen to like. If the conversation goes from whine to wine, you'll know you picked a few winners.

- Chardonnay
- Pinot noir
- Jordan cabernet sauvignon (It's the nectar of the gods.)
- Santa Margherita pinot grigio (If you really love your guests.)
- Seasonal wines: How about scheduling the party around the seasonal wine yield, like the fall merlots, perhaps?
- Sparkling and ice water: Have a few carafes available for guests who need to cool their jets on the wine.

PROPS AND DÉCOR

Use soft, low lighting to make guests feel comfortable enough to divulge some of their most humbling (albeit hilarious) moments.

MUSIC

- We won't stop you from choosing whatever music you want, but these songs would be funny as background music to your whining guests:
  - "Sixteen Tons" by Tennessee Ernie Ford
  - "In My Room" by the Beach Boys (It's where they took their crying and their sighing.)
  - Any country song: Something lousy always happens within the context of country music.
- If people get thoroughly depressed, play anything with an upbeat, happy tempo.

ENTERTAINMENT

- You will entertain one another as you all whine about the ironic moments in life. Make sure your guests know that you're out for laughter, so if someone has a really sensitive problem, he or she will know this isn't the time or the place to bring it up.

- If your guests need a little prodding, have them whine about a time when they unsuccessfully tried to get away with one of these common sins:
    - Duplicity
    - Tomfoolery
    - Hubris (See "Hubristic Tour" on page 127.)
    - Buffoonery
    - Shysterism
    - Cheapskatehood
    - Selfishness
    - Boorishness

- Your guests may even want to recount ironic tales involving the Big Seven:
    - Lust
    - Anger
    - Gluttony
    - Pride
    - Envy
    - Greed
    - Sloth

> If everyone ends up cracking up over stories like our Horse on Highway 10 tale, good for you. If Miss Crabapple takes the whining too seriously and drives the pathetic minutia of her life right into the ground, we suggest you nip the situation in the bud with the following prop: the whoopee cushion. With this little item, all you need to say to the filibusterer is "Here, have a seat while you finish your story." We did some research, and here's what the textbooks have to say:
>
>> Though its origins remain unknown, the red-colored, rubber-skinned, long-necked whoopee cushion *(Cushionus whoopus)* is recognized in all regions of North America. The whoopee cushion is conveniently sized and is easily transportable, which aids in camouflage and, ultimately, in its stealthy use. Its familiar and delightful call make it a favorite even today.

Story Weaver

A BLACK SATCHEL FELL OUT of the LIMO.

I PICKED UP THE SATCHEL.

THEN A BULLET WHIZZED OVER MY HEAD.!!

Gloria was expecting five or six dinner guests that evening. She knew they would speak of the murder, and it would give her the chance to convince them that she was not the last one to see Frank alive. She would ask them to RSVP by five. All she needed was a simple yes or no. If they agreed to come, she knew she would be safe—at least for a while.

If you hunger for spellbinding drama such as this and if you hunger for a good meal in the company of friends, you'll love our Story Weaver party. It offers succulent fare in terms of both feast and fiction. Right at your dinner table, you can resurrect the lost art of oral storytelling, something we ourselves enjoy more than a little. You can give your guests the rare opportunity to walk the sacred path of great oral-storytelling cultures, such as the Inuit and the Hopi. (Or not.)

For centuries, sharing food has lead to sharing thoughts. There must be something to the theory (the theory we just now made up) of how when food excites the taste buds, it gets the rest of the tongue moving, too. While the focus of this party is not food, your dinner table will be the forum for your guests to spin a yarn and weave it together while breaking bread.

INVITATION

By Phone

"Marge, today on my way home from the grocery store, I saw a black satchel fall out of a speeding limo. I swiftly pulled my car to the side of the road. I leaned down, picked up the satchel, and just then a bullet whizzed over my head!" Here's where you'll fall silent, compelling Marge to ask, "Goodness, what happened next?" Tell her, "I don't know. It's up to you. Join us tonight at seven for dinner and storytelling."

By E-Mail

Today on my way home from the grocery store, I saw a black satchel fall out of a speeding limo. I swiftly pulled my car to the side of the road. I leaned down, picked up the satchel, and just then a bullet whizzed over my head!

Join us tonight at 7:00 for dinner and storytelling, and you yourself can help piece together the exciting conclusion. Call John for details.

MENU

Dinner should have a comfy, easy feel. Use linens and generous-size napkins. Mix and match table settings for a colorful, pieced-together table. Use low centerpieces and candlelight.

Food

- Asian-flavored skirt steak: Marinate for at least a half-hour in ginger, garlic, brown sugar, sherry, soy, olive oil, cilantro, salt, and pepper, then broil.
- Ramen noodles: These come packaged with a flavor broth in which to cook them. (After cooking the noodles, reserve the broth.) Add a bit of Mongolian Fire Oil and a spoonful of peanut butter to the noodles. Toss before serving.
- Soup: Make this from the flavored broth you've reserved from the noodles. Add some finely chopped scallions.
- Cucumber salad: Chop cukes and red onions, and finely dice a jalapeño pepper. Dress with white rice vinegar sweetened with sugar. Add salt, pepper, and red pepper flakes to taste.
- Pound cake with vanilla ice cream: Drizzle a bit of piña colada mix over the top. Garnish with flaked coconut.

Beverages

- White Burgundy or sauvignon blanc
- Iced coffee or iced tea with dessert

PROPS AND DÉCOR

Have a tape recorder and a ninety-minute cassette available, and appoint someone as recording secretary. It will be fun to pull this story out and listen to it in another year.

MUSIC

We found that instrumental music works better than music with lyrics does. In the middle of a story, the last thing you'll need is a guest squealing, "Oh, I *love* this song!" And then there she'll be, singing along, trying to be real quiet so as not to distract others. But she *will* be distracting, and you may feel inclined to strike her. To avoid this problem, play music such as the following:

- Carl Doy on piano
- Michael Chapdelaine on guitar
- Greg Vail on saxophone

ENTERTAINMENT

Over dinner, you and your guests will create a story. Here's how it works:

- Go around the table and have each person add the next installment. If some guests are known to be long-winded, determine a time limit for each installment. However, if someone offers a thirty-second installment, and that's all she has, you'll have to respect that. (Since the storytelling will take place while people eat, it should be a bit easier for the wallflower to weave his tale because all eyes won't be riveted on him.)
- Go around the table as many times as it takes to bring the story to a natural conclusion. But we suggest you don't carry this out longer than forty-five minutes, or you'll see signs of people losing interest.
- To help you get going, we've made up a few story beginnings. Use these or make up your own. Or merely choose a literary genre and ask the first person to start that type of story, such as a Mickey Spillane-like gumshoe mystery, a Barbara Cartland-type heaving-bosom romance, a Hemingwayesque stream-of-consciousness adventure, or a real-life situation spun into the macabre, à la the creepmeister himself, Stephen King. Here's what we came up with:

- Once settled in the dreary Oregon fishing town, it took no time at all for Joe to become familiar with the liquor bottles in the bar at the end of Pier 45. In 1965, most bartenders weren't required to provide much beyond a strong martini and a discreet ear. And since that November day in Dallas in '63, discretion had become Joe's middle name. If only Tom hadn't given him the day off to watch the motorcade....

- Desperate to escape the consoling eyes of well-meaning friends after Brad's death, Amanda accepted Maggie and Jack's offer to use their beach house. While working on her fourth watercolor, Amanda idly watched a man struggling to get his Hobie Cat into the water. She returned to her painting, and the next time she looked up, she had lost sight of him. Sighing, she selected a brush and began mixing colors to capture the exact hue of the sea and the way it became more intense at the horizon. "Not bad," said a male voice behind her. She hesitated a second, then gathered up her materials, leaving the man puzzled as she hurried down the beach....

- In 1940, it was as easy as rolling down a hill to book a reservation from Miami to Lisbon on the clipper. It was the getting back that would prove to be tricky. But that fit perfectly with Burt's plan, now that he had Nina in Europe. Once they made their way into Burt's homeland, he would re-enlist in the Third Reich, and his wife, who had become such a burden to him, would simply vanish. Burt's inheritance from his rich socialite wife would never be questioned....

> Be forewarned: What the storytellers weave may surprise you. Our friends, who are always more than willing to be the canaries sent into our coal mines, allowed us to test this party on them, and they didn't give the stories the endings we'd hoped they'd give. Happy endings, it seems (at least judging from the grim stories our friends wove) come only out of Hollywood.

Pajama Game

When you hear what happened to our good friend, Barb, you'll understand perfectly why she hosted a pajama party at age forty-nine.

Barb's an all-around fun-loving gal, but she's also a brain, and from the day she graduated college, her career path headed directly into the conservative arena of banking. Presently, she's the human resources director at one of the major banks in our area, and during one fabulously gorgeous week in the middle of July, her bank forced her to attend an *insurance seminar!* She was devastated.

Tuesday through Friday we enjoyed the kind of weather that makes living in the Midwest worthwhile. And then there was Barb, enduring chilly air conditioning and fluorescent lights in a meeting room at a less-than-glamorous motel outside Peoria. For three-and-a-half days, her world centered on comparing and contrasting the benefits of term, whole, and universal life insurance as well as—*oh, blessed diversion!*—a lively discussion about annuities. Adding insult to injury, she also attracted the unwelcome attention of a middle-aged rep from Downstate Illinois Life and Casualty, the type of up-and-comer who rode into town on a smile and a shoeshine, like Arthur Miller's Willie Loman. By Wednesday night, Barb found herself praying for a tornado.

When at last Barb returned home that Friday night, the woman was most definitely ready to bust out. We managed to talk her out of doing anything illegal, and what she came up with instead was so much fun, we want to share it with you. It'll give you hope the next time you sit through that insurance seminar. Or condo association meeting. Or annual church conference. Because once you're released, you can have a pajama party, too!

INVITATION

We happen to think this party will be an absolute gas for women of any age, whether they're twenty-five or seventy-five. However, you can also pull it off as a coed event. (It's hard for us to imagine a group of men doing this solo, to be honest.) However you decide to go, it's the type of party you'll want to save for your closest friends, since we're guessing it would be unpleasant, at best, to see your boss or your minister in his pajamas.

By Phone

"Hi, this is Jane. I think it's time we slept together." (Use this invitation on men and women, since both will be equally shocked.)

By E-Mail

(Sing the following to the tune of the Rolling Stones' "Let's Spend the Night Together.")

Let's spend the night together.
Bring your pillow; make sure it's "feather."
Let's spend the night together! Now!

Shocked? Then call Jane for details.

MENU

Set up a junk-food buffet at night and an easy-to-make breakfast buffet in the morning. Use paper- or plasticware. (Nobody wants to do dishes at a slumber party!)

Food (Night)

Pajama party food includes anything that is positively yummy and absolutely terrible for you. But hey, you sat through that insurance seminar, so what's a little junk food in comparison?

- Popcorn sprinkled with Italian seasoning
- Pretzels and mustard
- Honey-roasted peanuts
- Cheese and crackers
- Potato chips
- Chee·tos
- Bridge mix

- Brownies or fudge: Be a sport. Let the guests make these. Everyone loves the smell of chocolate in the oven, and everyone likes to lick the bowl.

Beverages (Night)

- Bottled water: If you eat that much crud, do you really want to throw carbonation on top of it?
- Beer: In case carbonation is just what the doctor ordered.
- Blender drinks *(strong ones):* It's what Barb wanted at her party.

Food (Morning After)

Pick up these items the night before. No sense baking anything from scratch at six in the morning when you can warm ready-made yummies in the oven.

- Muffins
- Gourmet freezer waffles with fresh fruit, whipped cream, syrup, and flavored butters
- Sinfully delicious premade Belgian waffles: These come prebaked and vacuum-packed. Just unwrap them, warm them, and hit the confessional later.
- Toast or crusty French bread spread with warm all-fruit jam

Beverages (Morning After)

- Coffee (Maybe cinnamon flavored?): Ready the coffeemaker at night so the first person up need only flick the switch.
- Juice

PROPS AND DÉCOR

Make sure everyone has a place to sleep. Barb had everyone bring sleeping bags, pillows, and whatever else they needed to make the sleeping experience comfier. This party is more about novelty than about sleeping, but if you have any "egg crate" mattress padding, foam rubber, air mattresses, or cushions lying around, by all means, offer them up.

MUSIC

We suggest you listen to the same music you listened to the last time you attended a pajama party, which likely was when you were between eleven and fifteen years old. To accomplish this, have each guest bring any music they've managed to hold on to all these years. The artists will run the gamut, such as Frank Sinatra, Elvis Presley, Herman's Hermits, the Jackson Five, Men at Work, and U2. Weave these and music selections from other artists throughout the evening. Just stick with happy sounds and steer away from anything maudlin or headbanger.

ENTERTAINMENT

- When you have a three-hour party, you pull out the three-hour conversation. But you'll have more time at this party, and the conversations will become more telling. With the entire night to carry on, you'll form connections that you might expect to form at a retreat (but rarely *do*, we might add).

- Rent videos of cult classics, such as *Pulp Fiction, Blue Velvet, Austin Powers: International Man of Mystery, Saturday Night Fever, Splendor in the Grass,* anything by Hitchcock, *Easy Rider, The Manchurian Candidate, Singin' in the Rain,* or *The Seven Samurai*.

- Play board or card games, or tell fortunes with tarot cards.

- Remember when we'd get the "dialies" at three in the morning and call boys? Just wondering. Not that we'd *suggest* that sort of thing....

> When it comes to parties and to life in general, let it be known right this minute that we are all about freedom, justice, and equality for all. But there's one glaring exception: We have no problem whatsoever encouraging you to isolate all the snorers in one room. Ask each guest "Snorer or non?" early in the evening, so everyone can be gently shepherded into the proper sleeping quarters when the time comes. Because the last thing you'll want is a snorer crashing next to you when clearly she should be elsewhere.

Venus Flytrap

"Tall and tan and dark and handsome, Michael from Accounting goes walking, and as he passes, you smile—but he doesn't see...."

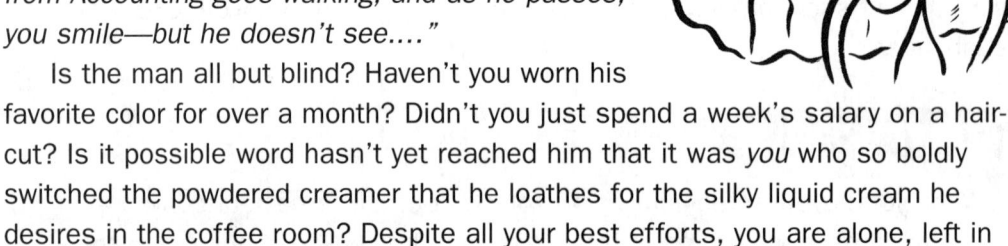

Is the man all but blind? Haven't you worn his favorite color for over a month? Didn't you just spend a week's salary on a haircut? Is it possible word hasn't yet reached him that it was *you* who so boldly switched the powdered creamer that he loathes for the silky liquid cream he desires in the coffee room? Despite all your best efforts, you are alone, left in the wake of his aftershave that leaves you weak in the knees. *Damn him!*

Courage, girls! Carefully follow the plan we shall delineate for you here, and love shall be yours. Men, this goes for you, too, aching as you are for the luscious lips of Pam from Personnel. (Should you desire the arms of Erique from Estimating, well, we guess it'll work, too.) We may aim the chapter at a woman longing after a man, but this party will work for anyone. So come closer, dears, as we reveal the magical secret of love.

Actually, it's more smoke and mirrors—and perhaps a dinner candle or two—than it is magic. We'll help you plan a deceptively simple and innocent dinner party, whereby you'll come off looking smashing, a little cosmopolitan, and every bit as complex as the Bordeaux. Though certainly subtler than a one-by-two delivered to the back of the head, à la *Cool Hand Luke*, the spirit of this party is essentially the same: *First you have to get their attention.* It's sneaky, it's clever, and it just might work!

INVITATION

In order for this party to fly, you'll need to invite friends (other than Michael) who promise to show up and act as "casual" guests. The last thing you'd want is a table of guests without Michael, but worse yet would be a table of no guests *but* Michael! Make sure your co-conspirators are a mixed bag to keep the seating arrangements from looking like "couple, couple, you, Michael." You don't need anything thing that spells *ambush*. After securing promises from the others, deliver a straightforward invitation to the *objet d'amour*. An e-mail invitation is too much of a wild card. You'll never know if he'll read his e-mail in time, so stick with the phone.

By Phone

"Michael, we're having drinks and dinner at my place at seven-thirty tonight. Can you join us?" If he can't give you a yes by two or three o'clock, save your energy. As a certain famous femme fatale once said, "Tomorrow is another day."

MENU

As you scan this section, we just bet you'll be completely overwhelmed. We normally wouldn't dream of including this many minute instructions and details, but there may be some uninitiated readers who have no experience whatsoever with entertaining or entrapment. This dinner party should showcase an easy, breezy you, so we'll show you how to pull off an evening of casual control, one step at a time.

Food

- Step 1—Prepare the meal: This menu is straightforward and elegant (not entirely unlike yourself) and will easily serve six. Even if you have to make a quick run to the grocery store, you can still prepare this meal with panache within two hours. We're not kidding.
  - Pork cutlets: Dip them in beaten egg, then dredge them in bread crumbs with Italian seasoning, salt, and pepper to taste. Brown these in butter in a sauté pan. They will cook quickly. Plan on two or three cutlets per person. Garnish with orange slices.
  - Side dish: Use packaged side dishes from the grocer. How about flavored rice? Curry rice works beautifully, and wild rice looks intriguing. Or go the Parmesan noodle route. Make the sauce sinfully rich by mixing the enclosed seasoning envelope with *all* milk (instead of half water, half milk, as the recipe calls for). If you have a red or green pepper, julienne-cut it, sauté it with the pork, and add it to the noodles at the last minute.
  - Vegetable: May we suggest baby carrots glazed with sherry and ginger? Microwave frozen baby carrots. Add several pats of butter and a scant handful of brown sugar. Add two shots of sherry and grated, powdered, or

candied ginger. Microwave them again until they are al dente, then adjust your seasonings.

- Rolls or bread loaves: Bring the bread piping hot to the table and place in a breadbasket lined with a large cloth napkin. Serve with honey butter. In a small bowl, slice butter into pats and drizzle with honey. Place a bowl of honey butter at both ends of the table. If you make honey margarine, whip the honey into the margarine and transfer to a clean serving bowl. Place the bowl on a small plate and rest a butter knife on the edge of the plate.

- Applesauce: It's great with pork. But don't put applesauce right on the plates. It'll run, and you want Michael to know you've thought of everything. Serve it in a bowl with a serving spoon.

- Green salad: Bagged salads will meet your time requirements. Add chopped Granny Smith apples, fresh zucchini, and a can of drained mandarin oranges to the greens. For a quick and impressive dressing, combine plain yogurt, horseradish brown mustard, and soft white vinegar, like rice vinegar. Sprinkle on Italian seasoning.

- Step 2—Set the table: Do this before guests arrive. It'll impress your guests (especially Michael) right off the bat. We'll give you a pass on the tablecloth or place mats, but generous-size cloth napkins are a must. When setting the table, place the salad plate on top of the dinner plate. Wrap a napkin around the silverware and place the bundle horizontally on top of the plates.

- Step 3—Dish up the food: Retrieve the dishes when it's time for dinner, and dish up the food in the kitchen. We're going to tell you how to arrange the food on the plate for maximum showmanship. Yes, yes, we realize this is getting trivial. However, you'll understand the reason for going the extra mile once you see the look on Michael's face as you deliver to him a quickly prepared, beautifully presented, and tasty bill of fare.

  - Spoon the rice into a horizontal strip across the center of the plate (from the nine o'clock to the three o'clock position).

  - Stagger the cutlets atop the rice, alternating them with orange slices.

  - Place the carrots at the twelve o'clock position, and add more orange slices at six o'clock.

  - If you have anything green and fresh, such as chives, use a bit atop the six o'clock oranges.

- Step 4—Serve dinner: Call the guests to the table as soon as is comfortable. Ask a male guest (not Michael) to help serve. (By the way, Miss Manners says, "Serve from the right. Remove from the left.") As people take their seats, resist the temptation to crawl onto Michael's lap. In fact, it's better if you don't even sit near him.

- Step 5—Clean the table: After dinner, do not fight people off if they want to help clear the table. Remember: Easy, breezy. Just say something like "Hey, great! While you do that, I'll make some coffee."

Beverages

Again, we lapse into minutia so you won't leave anything to chance. (Oh, don't bother to thank us. Just invite us to the wedding.)

- If you're truly a clever girl, you'll set up a bar in advance, which communicates to all (namely, to Michael) that you have scads of friends and scads of parties. Why, you entertain on a whim all the time (said the spider to the fly). Here's what you'll need:

  - Soda water
  - Tonic water
  - Vodka
  - Gin
  - Dark rum
  - Cola
  - Lemon-lime soda
  - French table wine
  - A good cabernet or merlot
  - Chilled bottled beer
  - Bottle opener
  - Cocktail napkins
  - Lemons and limes

- Have a wineglass and a water glass at each place setting. Likewise, have a pitcher of ice water on the table, and make sure the Bordeaux is open. After guests are seated, inquire who would like wine, and ask another guest (not Michael) to pour. If someone comes to the table with her predinner cocktail, for heaven's sake, you just let her. (After all, if Michael does this, you'll think it's absolutely adorable.)

- After dinner, ask a guest (again, not Michael) to look after the bar while you make coffee.

PROPS AND DÉCOR

- Once you've recovered from the shock that *"Michael is coming! Michael is coming!"* hide your flannel pajamas and tidy up the house.
- If you're using a flower centerpiece, keep it small. If you simply must use large flora, remove said large flora when you're ready for dinner.
- Set the lighting. When guests arrive, pools of soft, low lighting give a homey feel. Wait until dinner to light the candles on the table. After everyone is served, turn off the kitchen utility light. In fact, turn out all the other lights, so dinner is lighted by candlepower only.

MUSIC

Music will allow you to become multidimensional. Take not lightly this window to your soul. Select artists and songs that share the same pitch, so to speak, but yet run the gamut. Here are some examples:

- Tommy Dorsey as guests arrive: His music will fill the room with energy.
- Contemporary music during drinks: Make it move easy, like a Hootie and the Blowfish kind of thing. Or try something by Sarah McLachlan or Tori Amos.
- Classical pop during dinner: Try something by Frank Sinatra or vintage Latin jazz.
- After-dinner music: Here's when it could get interesting. Casually ask *Michael* to select something from your music collection. Now you'll get a chance to see what *he's* all about. Should he choose *Ride of the Valkyries* and seems pleased, say nothing. After all, compromise is a large part of love.

ENTERTAINMENT

Without medication, your guests may not be able to handle much more than dinner and cocktails. Besides, you'd hate to play some dopey board game when all you really want is *his* hand on your thigh! Stick with conversation, but steer it away from the office. Above all, do not morph back into the woman he encounters M–F, 8–5.

Remember, the plan is to chase your *objet d'amour* until *he* or *she* catches *you.* Your prey (in this case, Michael) will leave without having any clue whatsoever that the entire evening was a ruse intended solely to get him to notice you. With this casual approach, the pressure is off, and Michael can now feel comfortable calling on you, even if it's just as friends. *(For now!)*

Showtime!

Our friends have come to expect odd and unusual parties from us, so no one was a bit surprised when we hosted a talent show in our back yard. We asked each of our guests to prepare a short act to perform for the rest of the group. What they came up with had the rest of us screaming with laughter, gasping for air, and reaching for our inhalers. But before we get into the how-to of it, let us pass along the wisdom we gleaned from this party.

One of our guests took great pride in the act she created. She came in full regalia—a cow costume—and had a cassette of the Sons of the Pioneers singing "Don't Fence Me In." She planned to bounce out her act on our trampoline.

She got up on the trampoline, the music started, she happily bounced away, and the rest of the guests roared with laughter. Her face, peeping out between the black-and-white spots of her furry cow-head cap, reflected her delight as she realized she was bringing down the house. Then the unthinkable happened: Her husband, who had planned no act of his own, decided it looked like fun, so what did he do? He horned in on her act! He climbed onto the trampoline, and then the two of them were up there, bouncing and arguing to the point where the cowboy singing about the starry skies above could barely be heard.

The lesson we learned from hosting this party was crystal clear: Some guests don't want to perform, others do, and those who do don't necessarily want to share the spotlight. Be "udderly" certain that each cow has the pasture to herself, and you and your guests can milk this party for all it's worth!

INVITATION

By Phone

YOU: Five minutes, Mrs. Pierce.
THEY: Wh-what?
YOU: Well, actually, curtain call is eight tonight. I'm gonna make you a star, baby!

By E-Mail

When you least expect it, you're elected. You're the star today!

Curtain call is 8:00 tonight at [Your Name] Theater. Call for details.

MENU

Your menu will be what one might expect to see at a wrap party. Because your bill of fare will entirely consist of hors d'oeuvres, use your nicer-than-everyday serviceware and pass or place the food throughout the room.

Food

Hors d'oeuvres, dahling!: These come in all flavors and varieties, from crabmeat pastries to spinach pies and mini calzones. Buy them premade and frozen, and bake them in your oven for about twenty minutes. They are so incredibly simple, you won't believe it. And they taste as elegant as can be. (One box of hors d'oeuvres we purchased actually had a man wearing a tuxedo on it, and they tasted every bit as fancy as that box suggested they would!)

Beverages

May we suggest you have a "cocktail half-hour" prior to curtain call?

- Champagne, dahling!: If you have fluted or flat champagne glasses for the bubbly, wunnerful, wunnerful! If not, we're guessing no one will look down their noses if you use wineglasses.
- Cocktails, dahling!: Whatever your guests like to drink, let them have it. They may be looking for a little fortification prior to performance time.

PROPS AND DÉCOR

- Create a stage. This won't be nearly as elaborate as you may think. If you'll be outside, perhaps your deck can be the stage and your seating can be arranged on ground level. If you'll be indoors, your stage can be as simple as a doorway or the bathtub, if the logistics work. *Whoosh,* the shower curtain opens, and there stands Stanley Kowalski hollering for Stella.
- Illuminate the performer and turn down the rest of the lights. This can be easily accomplished by taking the shade off a floor lamp and placing the

lamp as close to the performer and as far from the audience as possible. You could also place a small lamp on the floor in front of the performer as a footlight. Hang white Christmas lights around a door or window frame to create the look of a theater marquee, or lay them along both sides of stairs to create the look of a lighted theater aisle.

- You'll need something that plays music. A boom box is fine for outdoors, but we're guessing you'll use a stereo system if you're indoors.

- Encourage guests to bring their own props and music. Otherwise, have various props and costume pieces available for the performers. No, don't rent costumes or anything like that. Just have some things in a box or basket that people can rummage through. We once took an acting class, and there was a woman who simply could not perform unless she was wearing a scarf on her head. It was odd as odd could be, but some of your guests may also feel more comfortable performing if they have costume pieces or props. Use anything you may have around the house: scarves, wigs, hats, hairpieces, cotton balls, bathrobes, peignoirs, pipes, eyeglasses, sunglasses, toys, pillows, soup ladles, flashlights, hobbyhorses, and so on.

- Set up a dressing room. In all likelihood, this will be your bathroom. Be a sport: Put a big star on the door.

MUSIC

Showtunes! Mix some Broadway musicals and soundtracks into whatever music your guests normally listen to. Most libraries carry old soundtracks, and the old ones are really funny: "You got to have a dreeeeeeeam! If you don't have a dreeeeeeeam, how you gonna have-a-dream-come-truuuuuuuue!"

ENTERTAINMENT

- When you invite your guests, ask them to prepare a short act. It can be a musical number (sung or lip-synched), dance number, reading, poem, soliloquy, and anything beyond. How about a rendition of Iron Butterfly's "In-A-Gadda-Da-Vida" drum solo? An imitation of the Church Lady from *Saturday Night Live* would be hilarity of the richest variety.

- Instead of having each guest prepare an act, you might want to hold "open auditions" for one act. You'll see five different interpretations of George C.

Scott's "kick the hell out of him" speech from *Patton* and as many versions of Bette Davis's Baby Jane goofiness.

- Guests can't think of anything to do? You'll think of something *for* them! This may require a little chutzpah, but speaking for ourselves, we had no problem popping in an Elvis CD, taping sideburns to a guest, and letting her know she wouldn't have to lip-synch "I'm just a hunk-a, hunk-a burning love" if she had come up with an act of her own. Try as they might, no one escaped scot-free at our Showtime! party. (But use your judgment here. If Mr. Peepers adamantly refuses, just leave him be. Our number one rule when it comes to entertaining is that everyone must feel comfortable. You'll know how far you can push your guests.)

- The acts can be done solo or in tandem. Be sure to determine in advance if anyone will be performing together. (See "horning in" scenario on page 153.)

- As guests arrive, find out what they'll be doing, and then determine the order in which they'll be performing. (There'll always be that one guy who wants to be serious. Leave it to him to relive tenth grade English by performing the "Friends, Romans, Countrymen" bit from *Julius Caesar*. Put this guy on first.)

- Once the acts begin, keep them to a maximum time limit of two or three minutes. If someone's going too long, flash the lights to indicate that it's time to wrap 'er up.

- If anyone balks and decides not to come to the talent show, let them know in no uncertain terms that you'll hunt them down like the dogs they are. Consider these variations:

    - Your friend can't come and perform at eight? No problem! Tell her you'll be over at three with a video camera to tape her performance. Then show the tape at the party.

    - If Muhammad won't come to the mountain, then the mountain will come to Muhammad! Feel free to schlep everyone over to see the person who "couldn't get a baby sitter." Then let him do his performance in his own home. See how he likes doing *that* in front of his kids, God, and everyone!

> We're not suggesting your guests have to show up with a guitar or tap shoes in hand. This is not *Star Search*. We don't even expect your guests will be particularly talented. In fact, the less talent they have, the funnier they will be.

Hot Wax Night

We have a question. And if anyone can answer it, would you please post your response on www.we_don't_get_it.com? Because we are simply unable to wrap our brains around the concept of "air guitar."

Would someone explain what prompts adults—in this case, it's completely accurate to say *men*—to debase themselves by mimicking a rock star playing a guitar? We have observed men playing imaginary guitars and taking great pains to strategically position their fingers in what they imagine the correct chord arrangements to be. But here's the real kicker: We know for a fact that these men have *never taken even one single guitar lesson in their entire lives!* (If you could only hear how high-pitched our voices sound right now.)

Whereas we hope "air guitar" is on the decline, we hope the music that inspires it is here to stay. This party is about the dawn of rock 'n' roll, and you'll play all your favorites. Just make sure your selections hold to the Dick Clark rule of thumb: It's gotta have a good beat so you can dance to it.

Note: In none of those early Elvis or Buddy Holly performances have we *ever* seen a fan playing air guitar. Hopefully, at your Hot Wax Night, neither will you.

INVITATION

By Phone

"Karen, pull out that poodle skirt—you know, the one that makes your waist look so tiny! We're gonna rock around the clock tonight at eight!"

By E-Mail

We're gonna rock around the clock tonight at 8:00! Bring your music collection and spin us a hit!

Call George by 5:00.

MENU

Don't go anywhere fancy with this malt shop menu. Serve on paper- or plasticware and use paper napkins.

Food

- Hamburgers: Grilled or broiled and served preassembled on buns. Have condiments such as ketchup, mustard, pickle relish, diced onions, tomatoes, lettuce, and avocado slices. Just a suggestion: Have several bottles of ketchup available. It's so tiresome to be standing in line, balancing a plate for what seems like an eternity, watching someone shake the ketchup bottle, waiting—just *waiting!*—for him to make some lame joke just so you know it's the *ketchup's* fault that it's not coming out of the bottle! (Get those squeeze bottles, and this kind of thing will be headed off at the pass anyway.)
- Tater Tots or their even crispier cousins, Crispy Crowns: We're not going to ask you to deep-fry any French fries. These can be popped into the oven and served with ketchup for a really close replica.
- Individual bags of potato chips: Connect several skirt hangers to make a "ladder" and clip the bags on both sides. Hang this chip display near the condiment table.
- Soda fountain creations: Make malts with any flavor ice cream, milk, and malt powder. Have maraschino cherries, bananas, nuts, and syrups for those who wish to create sundaes and banana splits.

Beverages

- Coke or 7 UP in small glass bottles with straws
- A bowl of fruit punch: Make sure this is a boffo, orangish-pink color, even if you have to add food coloring. Early in the evening, give the baddest of the bad boys a bottle of rum or vodka, and ask him to spike the punch.

PROPS AND DÉCOR

The décor uses the types of items that would have been used to transform that high-school gymnasium into "An Evening in Venice." (*We* were fooled! Weren't *you* fooled?) You know the stuff:

- Paper flowers
- Twisted crepe paper streamers hung from the edges of the ceiling to meet at the center of the room
- A few of those expandable, honeycomb, multicolored party balls
- Paper tablecloths
- Candles in glass bowls surrounded by waxy white netting
- Mr. Microphone or any type of inexpensive broadcasting apparatus
- A good sound system: Here's where you'll appreciate that CD changer.

MUSIC

Encourage guests to bring their favorite fifties rock 'n' roll tunes. As long as it's danceable, you can be flexible. Try anything from Bill Haley and the Comets' 1955 classic "Rock Around the Clock" to the Temptations' 1965 hit "My Girl." Here are more examples to get you pointed in the right direction:

- "Hound Dog" by Elvis Presley
- "Wake Up Little Susie" by The Everly Brothers
- "At the Hop" by Danny and the Juniors
- "Tequila" by The Champs
- "Venus" by Frankie Avalon
- "Runaway" by Del Shannon
- "The Twist" by Chubby Checker
- "Johnny Angel" by Shelley Fabares
- "Sherry" by Frankie Valli and the 4 Seasons
- "Hey Paula" by Paul & Paula
- "He's So Fine" by The Chiffons
- "I Want to Hold Your Hand" by The Beatles
- "Chapel of Love" by The Dixie Cups
- "I Get Around" by The Beach Boys
- "Oh Pretty Woman" by Roy Orbison
- "Downtown" by Petula Clark

- "This Diamond Ring" by Gary Lewis and the Playboys
- "Mrs. Brown You've Got a Lovely Daughter" by Herman's Hermits

ENTERTAINMENT

This party will work equally well indoors or out. The focus is certainly music and dancing, but here are a few ideas to make it even campier:

- Pull out Mr. Microphone and announce the spotlight dance! Who can forget those five lucky *Bandstand* couples who got to be in the spotlight? Get out flashlights and blind your spotlight couples away, we say!
- Give guests each a number as they arrive, and call out Bingo Dancing to create couples. Pull the numbers out of a box. "Dancer number two and dancer number seven!"
- Pass fruit under the chin. This was always good for titillation and a little *tee hee* at a sock hop.
- Oh, those crazy kids! Weren't the adults just shaking their heads over pranks like the black-teeth gum, the bug in the ice cube, the rubber hot dog, the laughing toilet seat? Yes, these gags are goofy, but we think they'll add to the ambiance.
- Have at it with the goldfish swallowing, the clown-car antics, the phone booth stuffing if you want, but we draw the line when it comes to the chicken fight. Women perched on the shoulders of men, with the intent of knocking one another off, should scream "Danger, Will Robinson!" to all but the most dim-witted among us, don't you think?

> Sure as we are that there was no "air guitar" in the early era of rock 'n' roll, surely there must have been "air surfboard." What else are we to think when we see close-ups of Frankie Avalon surfing in all those beach movies? He was supposed to be hangin' ten, but you know darned well he was standing on a chair in a lot at MGM. Behind him, a bad projection image showed a wave that could only be described as a tsunami. And there he was, smiling away. When you're playing those groovy surfin' tunes at your Hot Wax Night, that "air surfboard" may just make a cameo appearance. If so, welcome it as good, clean fun. But slam the door in the face of anything that shows signs of transforming itself into "air guitar." *(The horror! The horror!)*

New Blood

This party is just the ticket if your social circle has the circumference of a fishbowl. Old friends are pure gold, but after hearing eighteen times running about the trip to Big Sur, it's not a bad idea to consider casting a large, wide net to snag some new friends.

New Blood requires your regular guests to bring a person or a couple the rest of the group has not previously met. A few hours into this party, you'll have gotten to know an entirely new group of people while on your own turf. And *those* people will certainly know *other* people. It's like that old shampoo commercial: "You'll tell two friends, and they'll tell two friends, and so on, and so on." Besides meeting new people, you'll also spend the entire evening sampling new and different foods, beverages, and music your guests are eager to share.

So what will you find in your net? Will you find a nice grouper or salmon? Or might there be a barracuda or two? A mahi-mahi? And don't forget, there just might be a grain of sand residing within that oyster shell, so don't be too hasty to toss it back into the sea—just enjoy the catch.

INVITATION

By Phone

It's probably best to give a day's notice for this party, because it does require your guests to do a bit more than just pop over on a whim. Your invite might go something like this: "Doris, they say everyone in the world is only six people away from knowing everyone else in the world. Tomorrow night, we're going to remove another degree of separation." Then ask Doris to bring a friend you have not met before as well as an unusual dish or beverage and a music selection.

By E-Mail

It is said that six degrees of separation keep us from being friends with everyone on planet Earth. Tomorrow night, we're going to remove one degree.

Contact Jack and Juanita for details.

MENU

La dolce vita accurately describes this party. It allows a nibble here and a sip there—the tasting of life and the friends, food, drink, and music it brings. Because this is a sampling party, you'll need sample-size cups, plates, plasticware, and quality paper napkins. You'll also need a number of platters and bowls for the dishes the guests will contribute. Let your guests know it's A-Okay if they need to prepare or warm their foods in your kitchen. Be sure to stagger the buffet offerings so everything isn't served at once.

Food

You yourself will add a new dish to the buffet, but the beauty of this party is that your guests will bring the rest of the food. When you ask your friends to bring a dish, here are some categories you might steer them toward:

- Hors d'oeuvres: The workhorse of the buffet table.
- Cheeses with crackers or toast points
- Sausages and cold meats
- Rice dishes
- Raviolis with unusual stuffing
- Smoked fish
- Pâtés
- Dips and sauces
- Marinated fruits
- Breads
- Desserts: *Exciting* is how we would describe ten pints of Ben & Jerry's next to little plastic cups and spoons. Pig Heaven, open the gates!

Beverages

Again, you will add one beverage to the buffet, but here are some ideas you can pass along to your guests:

- Wines: How divine, to spend an evening sampling a variety of unusual wines.
- Beers: You can use what's left over from the ever popular "Munich Meets Milwaukee" party. (See page 131.)
- Flavored essence water
- Bottled iced coffee

PROPS AND DÉCOR

- Adjust your lighting according to the time of day. For us, there's nothing better than sunshine. However, if you have this party in the evening, you'll want just enough lighting for guests to discern the food. You can achieve this effect with a mix of candles and table lamps with low-watt bulbs.
- Make sure you have discreet containers for disposal.
- Provide note cards and pens so guests can label what they brought for the buffet.

MUSIC

The preparation for this party just keeps getting better and better and easier and easier. Each of your guests will bring a CD he or she would like to share. Guests may bring their favorites, or they may bring unusual selections the group has not heard before. To make sure the CDs will be returned to their proper owners, encourage this church potluck practice: Have each guest write his or her name on a piece of masking tape and affix it to the CD case.

ENTERTAINMENT

Here are some games to play early in the evening or incrementally throughout the party. They are great icebreakers designed to give you more to talk about than what's in the dip.

- What's My Line?: Remember that game show with Dorothy Kilgallen and Arlene Francis? At your party, each new person will be introduced by his "sponsor" friend, and the rest of the guests will guess his occupation. Ask yes-or-no questions—such as "Are you in a service industry?" or "Are you in the medical field?"—until the person's occupation or avocation is figured out.

- Six Degrees of Kevin Bacon: This popular parlor game, created by three Albright College frat brothers, is based on the theory that any given celebrity can be connected to actor Kevin Bacon in six degrees or fewer. Here's an example: Connect Richard Chamberlain to Kevin Bacon. 1) Richard Chamberlain was in *The Thornbirds* with Barbara Stanwyck; 2) Barbara Stanwyck was in *Roustabout* with Elvis; 3) Elvis did *King Creole* with Walter Mathau; 4) Walter Mathau was in *JFK* with Kevin Bacon. You can use a celeb other than Kevin Bacon, and you can make up your own rules, allowing for connections through movies, marriages, relationships, or whatever you like.

> If you end each weekend reflecting, "I have *got* to make new friends," this party cleverly disguises your desperation as confidence. As your guests gush, "Oh, it must be *terribly* nerve-wracking to invite *sooo* many people you've never even *met* before!" your response can be delivered with assurance as you make your way to that most interesting-looking creature on the other side of the room. "Excuse me, dear," you can say, "there's someone I haven't welcomed yet."

Radio Days

Those of us who came into the world during or after the dawn of television are too young to remember the golden age of radio. What we missed by being born too late was an opportunity to participate in the theater of the mind. Well into the fifties, entertainment for much of America was an evening gathered around the radio. Via the theater of the mind, listeners were carried to a place far from their living rooms. With captured breath and some hand-holding, listeners became giddy with fear. Or howled with laughter. Or contemplated the history-making speeches of a world at war.

Come with us now as we step back in time. Close your eyes and imagine: Ladies in dresses, gentlemen in suits…We're sipping a glass of sherry as we wait for tonight's broadcast…As the radio warms up, we hear the first crackle of static…The year is 1940….

INVITATION

By Phone

"Cheryl, can you join us at six-thirty tonight for cocktails and dinner? At eight, we'll listen to the broadcast direct from London. Winnie's giving his 'We Shall Fight on the Beaches' speech. The year is 1940, so dress accordingly."

By E-Mail

George and I are playing up the nostalgia of old radio shows tonight. We'll serve cocktails and a buffet supper at 6:30. The broadcast of "War of the Worlds" begins at 8:00. It's 1940, so dress accordingly.

Kindly phone Trish by 3:00.

MENU

Buffets were styled a bit differently then than they are today. Use your good tableware and linens. Arrange the silverware and folded napkins in a staggered pattern. Use the cake as the centerpiece. We offer two types of menus depending on the season in which you'll host the party. The winter menu is perfect when you're cozied up in the living room. The summer repast is perfect when you're in your screened porch and the night air settles upon the back of your neck.

Winter Food

- Cold roast beef with horseradish sauce
- Corn succotash
- Garlic and cheddar mashed potatoes
- Parsnips browned in butter
- Crusty French bread with butter
- Chocolate layer cake

Summer Food

- Cold roast beef with dijonnaise sauce
- Roasted garlic potato salad with red onion and freshly ground pepper
- Corn on the cob steamed in the microwave with a pass of salt and butter
- Crusty French bread: Make dipping sauce by blending cilantro (or roasted red pepper), garlic, and olive oil. Serve at room temperature.
- Chocolate layer cake

Winter Beverages

- Hot toddy
- Hot mulled wine
- Whiskey sour
- Scotch and soda
- Brandy old-fashioned
- Gibson

- Bull Shot: Combine liquid beef bullion, vodka, Worcestershire sauce, a splash of Tabasco, and a squeeze of lemon.

Summer Beverages

- Brandy Alexander
- Champagne cocktail
- Gertie's Garter: Combine gin, grenadine, and grapefruit juice to taste.
- Bloody Mary
- Gimlet
- Silver Stallion: Combine gin, vanilla ice cream, and lemon and lime juice.

PROPS AND DÉCOR

Create a nostalgic glow with low-watt incandescent lighting. Use lamps, possibly even a few small bedroom lamps, rather than overhead lighting. Use these at the buffet as well as in your cocktail and entertainment areas.

MUSIC

During cocktail hour and the buffet, play those great World War II favorites. If you can find both American and European recordings, all the better. You can easily find forties CDs and tapes at the library or any music store. Here are a few artists:

- Glenn Miller, the icon of his time
- Tommy Dorsey
- Jimmy Dorsey
- The Andrews Sisters
- Benny Goodman
- Lionel Hampton
- Sammy Kaye
- Gene Krupa
- Guy Lombardo
- Freddy Martin
- Duke Ellington
- Nat King Cole
- Edith Piaf, Charles Trenet, and others on *Paris After Dark*

ENTERTAINMENT

- Hopefully, you'll lead your guests into behaving "as if"—in this case, as if it's 1940. Back then, society was polite, manners were observed, and language was watched. If everyone makes a bit of effort to dress the part, acting the part will come naturally.

- Begin the evening by inviting guests into the "parlor" (wherever that happens to be for you) for music and cocktails. After a half-hour, offer your buffet.

- After the buffet is served, invite guests into the "drawing room" (previously used as the "parlor"). Settle everyone in with coffee or a fresh cocktail, and then slip back in time with an old-time radio program. Your library will likely have at least a few of these selections. Others are available through "Wireless," the National Public Radio catalog, or through several web sites. Here are some examples:

> The year 1940 did not know the miracle of broad-spectrum antibiotics, laser surgery, the Internet, intercontinental phone service, soft contact lenses, or affordable air travel. It was a time when we were just coming out the Depression, and the entire planet was in the grips of a worldwide cataclysm. And yet, life *was* simpler in that bygone era, wasn't it? People seemed to know what it meant to have enough. During the golden age of radio, it was enough to spend an evening with friends, enjoy good food and drink, and listen to works of audio art that were destined to stand the test of time.

- The Man Called X
- Adventures of Ellery Queen
- The Adventures of Philip Marlowe
- The Adventures of Sherlock Holmes
- The Avenger
- The Burns and Allen Show
- Captain Midnight
- CBS Radio Workshop
- Dimension X
- Inner Sanctum Mysteries
- The Jack Benny Program
- Mr. Keene, Tracer of Lost Persons
- My Little Margie
- Our Miss Brooks
- The Saint
- The Shadow
- The Adventures of Superman
- Tarzan of the Apes
- Tom Mix
- Yours Truly, Johnny Dollar

- We suggest no more than thirty to forty-five minutes for listening. Longer than that, the natives could get restless. Put the music back on, freshen the cocktails, and be admonished by Patty, Maxine, and LaVerne as they warn you not to sit under the apple tree with anyone else but them.

168

Okay, but Not at My House!

How often does something like this happen? You spend all day cleaning the house and yard, and the place looks so fabulous you can hardly stand it. You're well aware that by tomorrow, your preschoolers, teenagers, or dog will have the place looking like it did this morning, before you began your domestic blitzkrieg. You want to have people over *right now*, but since you've spent the entire day cleaning, there's no time to cook dinner!

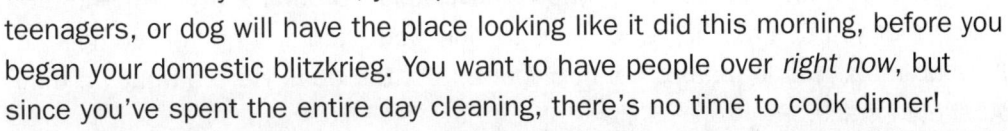

Or how about this? You cook the most fabulous, creative, and delicious meal you have ever, ever, *ever* concocted in your long-legged life! You're dying to show off your culinary prowess *this minute!* But the house looks like the aftermath of a natural disaster. How to solve that age-old problem of *clean house/no food* or its mirror image, *great dinner/pigpen house*? We have an idea. Let us share.

One day one of us (who shall remain nameless because she apparently had a pigpen house) called the other of us and said this: "Hello, ——? Hi, honey, it's ——! What would you say if I made a wonderful dinner tonight and invited over some mutual friends? Hmm? How does that sound? Sounds good? Great! All you have to do is have it at *your* house!

After the shock of such unabashed chutzpah wore off, dinner was agreed upon. One of us did all the cooking; the other agreed to take care of music and candles, set a table, and open the doors to her spic-and-span home. However your evening comes together, the point here is that each host gets to capitalize on what she or he has to offer. What's not to love?

INVITATION

Either you or your partner will invite the guests—just make darned sure you both like everyone on the guest list.

By Phone

"Charlene, it's Anna. I'm inviting you to dinner tonight at seven at Kathleen's house...Oh, never you mind why! We'll explain the whole story tonight!"

By E-Mail

You are invited for a fabulous dinner tonight at 7:00 at the home of our friend Kathleen.

RSVP to Anna before 5:00.

MENU

If you'll be the cook tonight, you won't have to worry about décor or music, so we're going to make you cook like you've never cooked before! If your friend is willing to let you use her home for entertaining, you shouldn't pull off some kind of prefab meal. You'll need to hold up your end of the deal. Here's what we think you should make:

Food

- Barbecued or broiled flank steak: Rub in salt, pepper, garlic, and Worcestershire sauce really well. Broil 6–7 minutes on each side. Slice *thinly* on the *bias*. (Why the italics, you ask? Because it's important.) Serve with a *chimichurri* sauce.
- Seasoned breadsticks: Use packaged crescent rolls. Roll them out and slice into strips. Roll strips in seasoning of your choice, like oregano and Parmesan. Twist and lay them on a cookie sheet. (You can prepare these ahead of time, cover with plastic wrap, and keep them refrigerated.) Just prior to serving, bake until brown.
- Pesto mashed potatoes: Prepare mashed potatoes. During the last minutes of whipping, add pesto, salt, and pepper.
- Endive with citrus and tomato salsa: You'll need one endive head per guest. Cut off the bottom (just above the core) and separate the leaves. The canoe-shaped leaves simply beg to be filled then eaten by hand. We suggest adding a small, chopped Granny Smith apple and a can each of drained sweet corn and black beans to your favorite salsa. Season to taste, including a dash of

cumin. Spoon filling into the leaves just before serving. Squeeze on a bit of fresh lime juice.

- Seasonal fruit and *crème anglaise* fondue: In advance, cut fruit into bite-size pieces that can be skewered. Crème anglaise can be served cold or warmed in the microwave. You can make a mock crème anglaise by using Cool Whip, pure vanilla extract, a little brown sugar, and some rum. Serve each guest an individual bowl of fruit and crème anglaise.

We *told* you we would send you a bit over the top, didn't we?

Beverages

- Chardonnay and beer prior to dinner
- Merlot and cabernet sauvignon or ice water with lime with dinner
- Champagne with peach schnapps, or coffee (hot or iced) after dinner

PROPS AND DÉCOR

If you're not cooking, you'll have plenty of time to gather a few things to make your clean house even more special.

- How about picking up some flowers for the table?
- Small votive candles at each place setting are simple, pretty, and can rest safely on china saucers.

MUSIC

When it comes to home entertaining, perhaps there has been no greater advancement than the "shuffle" feature included on many CD players. But other great jewels are the mixed CDs offered in Pottery Barn, import stores, or discount stores. They include great selections that are not readily available. We've provided a few samples of what we think works well for this dinner party. Whether you make your selections from this list or draw them from your own collection, pick a variety of music that shares the same feel and intensity.

- *Heat Wave* from Pottery Barn, featuring
    - Harry Belafonte;
    - Benny Moré;

- Astrud Gilberto;
- Tito Puente;
- And, believe it or not, Desi Arnaz and His Orchestra!

• *Rhythms in Common* from Cost Plus World Market, featuring
- Majek Fashek (African reggae);
- Maxi Priest (reggae);
- Angelique Kidjo (African world beat);
- Les Nubians (French pop);
- Michael Doucet & Cajun Brew (Cajun);
- Peter Tosh (reggae).

ENTERTAINMENT

Enjoy the company of friends, enjoy the wine, and enjoy the good food and clean home that you two so craftily combined.

> The whole concept of this party is... well, it's genius. Especially if you live near each other, we can't think of an easier way to give a dinner party. For the cook and the home-owner, there's just no downside. No doubt peanut butter and jelly began with just such genius.

Happy Trails to You!

Is there a buckaroo among you who's about to ride off into the sunset? Retire? Move? Transfer to a new location? Or merely move to a new department? Each and every one of these circumstances is a perfect excuse to host our Happy Trails party.

In this chapter, we focus our efforts on a retirement party, simply because we find so many retirement parties to be pretty doggone lame. People always feel compelled to pull out one of two themes: *golf* or *fishing*. Not us, no sir. We send the ol' cowpoke out to pasture, gnawing on a barbecued rib and doing the Texas two-step.

This is one of our easiest parties. It takes very little to create a western theme because the smell of barbecued ribs will take you out of wherever you happen to be and place you smack dab in the middle of the Longbranch Saloon. Move over, Miss Kitty!

INVITATION

By Phone

"Alicia, that ol' cowpoke Andy Hanahan is fixin' to hang up his spurs! Can you join us tonight at seven so we can take him out for one last ride?"

By E-Mail

Howdy, Pardners!

Our fellow buckaroo, Andy Hanahan, is hangin' up his spurs. Join us tomorrow night at 7:00 as we take him for one last ride before he heads out to pasture.

Call Kathy by 4:00 for details.

MENU

Food

- Barbecued ribs: Either pull out the grill and open the doors so the smell can permeate your house, or do them in the oven. The trick is to cook them slowly so the climax of your party will be y'all sittin' down to eat barbecue. If you're *really* pressed for time, have the ribs delivered or pick them up from a local barbecue restaurant. As we said earlier, the barbecue smell makes much of the ambiance, so you'll need to create the aroma even if you don't cook. We don't think they make "barbecue" air fresheners yet, so light some kind of a fire and toss on mesquite wood chips.
- Corn bread: Add a few jalapeño peppers to a "Jiffy" corn muffin mix.
- Baked beans from the deli or the jar: Dress them up with crumbled bacon.
- Cole slaw: Again, hit the deli or the barbecue restaurant. Chicken places also make great slaw.
- Brownies, apple pie, or some dessert a cowboy would love

Beverages

- Beer
- Soda
- Hearty red wine: A merlot would be great with barbecued ribs.
- Strong coffee after the meal

PROPS AND DÉCOR

Didn't we tell you this was easy? Very little can compete with that barbecue smell wafting through your house. But if you have time, you may want to include the following:

- Gingham-checked tablecloth: Gingham is $1.98 a yard at a fabric store, so if you haven't the inclination to hunt for a real tablecloth, just drape fabric over the table.
- "Wanted" poster: If you have time, it would be funny to get a photo of your honoree blown up into poster size. Write something below the photo, such as

"WANTED: For having too much fun during retirement" or some such goofiness. There's no need for this to be a particularly attractive photo, mind you.

MUSIC

All country, all the time. Artists include the following:

- Vince Gill
- LeAnn Rimes
- Dixie Chicks
- Clint Black
- Garth Brooks
- Reba McEntire
- Shania Twain
- Willie Nelson
- Patsy Cline
- Hank Williams

ENTERTAINMENT

The ribs and the music should keep you more than entertained. But at some point in the evening, you'll want to give all glory, laud, and honor to the departing cowpoke. This can be accomplished in a couple different ways:

- Funeral: Eulogize your "dearly departing." Much like Tom Sawyer, he'll have the pleasure of attending his own funeral. Each guest will be allowed to say a few words about the honoree. Someone may even lament, "Oh, he always *loved* barbecued ribs!"

- Roast: Yep, roast him as surely as you'd roast a side of beef on a spit. Let him have it from all directions (as long as it's all in good fun, of course). In advance, ask each of your guests to prepare a story about the honoree. The story should be embarrassing or something he'd care to forget (but still in good taste). After he's well-done, each person can offer something kind to say as well.

> Now, we are not the type to suggest you do something wicked, but if we *were*, we happen to think this would be the perfect party to host when someone crappy finally gets the hell out of your life. Obviously, your "honoree" won't attend the party, so you can forget about saying anything kind about him. (Saying anything cathartic is more fitting.) The western theme will still work; instead of envisioning him riding off into the sunset, you can think about him heading off to the gallows at high noon.

Vice-Free Party

You've painted up your lips and rolled and curled your tinted hair.... The old song does not say how Ruby felt the morning after she took her love to town. But we can guess.

We're talking about that feeling everyone gets the morning after a night of bad behavior. In our circle, the guilt one heaps upon oneself after the fact is known as the "Stone of Shame." It's a conceptual trophy that passes from person to person, and we've all had it at one time or another. Let us share the story of how the present trophy-bearer earned the award and what she decided to do about it.

Keeping with our theme, we'll just call her "Ruby." Her misadventure took place at the Crawfish Festival in Lemont, Illinois. Ruby joined us as a single, her husband being unable to go. Now, Ruby is only five-foot-two, but that night, she put away enough red, red wine to knock a bull on its behind. The deterioration of her behavior was directly proportional to the amount of alcohol that crossed her once-sweet lips, and to keep from *completely* ruining her reputation, that's all we're going to say about that.

The following day, Ruby's husband received a phone call. "Lemont?" she heard him say. Her eyes became as big as saucers, thinking that her past had caught up with her, that some official from the town in which her shenanigans took place felt compelled to report her behavior. The relief she felt when she realized it was merely Lemont Smith, her husband's business colleague, and *not* the long arm of the Lemont law, prompted her to create the party that follows.

The Vice-Free Party allows the person bearing the Stone of Shame to test the waters and make sure she is still accepted by friends. But you don't have to wait till you're bearing the Stone to host this party. In fact, chances are you *won't* be bearing the Stone of Shame when you decide to have this vice-free get-together, because this is just good, clean fun for the whole family. This is the kind of party you can throw at any time, for no reason whatsoever, and it's so squeaky clean, you can even invite the kidlets or your minister.

176

INVITATION

By Phone

"John and I are just hanging out. Wanna come hang with us? Maybe play some games and have some sandwiches?"

By E-Mail

How's about you and _____ comin' on over at _____? We're gonna serve up some _____. Bring the young'uns!

MENU

Haul out paper- or plasticware, and just let everyone have at it.

Food

We're seeing "sammiches" for this party. What's not to love about a sandwich, especially when you can make your own? It couldn't be easier, and everyone gets exactly what he or she likes. Have plenty of the following fixins available:

- Bread: Pick up loaves of French bread or whole-grain breads from a bakery or grocery store.
- Cheese: Get presliced Swiss, provolone, Gouda, or brick. Have some American on hand if there'll be little ones in attendance.
- Cold cuts: Hit the deli and have them slice up thin cuts of roast beef, smoked turkey breast, ham, and salami.
- Garnishes such as pickles, olives, red onion slices, tomatoes, sprouts, and lettuce leaves
- Condiments such as mayonnaise, mustard, horseradish, oil and vinegar, and herbs (chopped green onions, cilantro, basil, and oregano)
- Potato chips: You say you're on your best behavior, so now let's see you eat just one.
- Desserts: What could be more wholesome and all-American than ice-cream cones? Or how about a freshly baked fruit pie? Cherry, apple, and blueberry practically have us saluting the flag and singing the praises of motherhood.

Beverages

- Soda
- Coffee
- Iced tea
- Sparkling water
- Milk shakes!

PROPS AND DÉCOR

You won't need much of anything for just hangin'. It really depends on the season:

- If it's summer, pull out some blankets or towels for a picnic or so the kids can play on the grass. Or bring out the lawn chairs and picnic tables. The dress code is anything that goes well with bare feet.
- If you're hanging out while there's a blinding snowstorm raging outside, wear your big socks or slippers. If you have a fireplace, now's the time to get cozy in front of a roaring blaze.

MUSIC

- You don't want to put on anything that smacks of sin and vice, so you may want to save the *wha-wha-wha* of the sax for another time. Think fun, happy, and wholesome, such as music from the following artists:
    - The Beach Boys
    - Sly and the Family Stone
    - Hootie and the Blowfish
    - Sting
    - Crosby, Stills, Nash and Young
    - Goo Goo Dolls
- Let us tell you how Ruby handled the music issue at her own party. She wanted to show us she could behave just fine, thank you very much, when surrounded by the same music that got her all frisked up that fateful night in Lemont. So she played music by the same group that played at the Crawfish Festival, just to show us that she could indeed remain a model of decorum

while listening to Mojo and the Bayou Gypsies. How could we possibly not welcome her back into the fold?

ENTERTAINMENT

- Get some outdoor games going:
  - Badminton
  - Volleyball
  - Baseball
  - Croquet

- Or if you're indoors, try these:
  - Monopoly
  - Risk
  - Scrabble
  - Pictionary

- Or how about this? You really don't have to do *anything*. And yes, we readily acknowledge you can figure that out for yourselves, so don't sass us with, "Well, *we* could have thought of *that!*" We're giving you the thumbs up to do something you may otherwise have thought was lame—so you just put that in your pipe and smoke it.

> This party is our way to reintroduce the concept of "just hanging" without having to have a plan of action in mind. Sometimes, all you really want to do is spend time with friends. After all, when you hung out when you were young, you didn't give much thought to the fact that you weren't doing much or even doing anything. And there must have been something to that lack of thought, because hanging was something you did quite often once upon a time. Besides, an afternoon like *this* after a night like *that* is just what is needed in order to feel accepted again.

Virtual Party

Ah, the Internet! Where else can *reality* turn into *virtual reality* with the click of a mouse? Most aspects of real life can be found in some virtual form on the Internet. Think about it:

- You've got playground politics among the "buddies" on your instant messaging (IM) service. "So-and-so has me *blocked*—can you believe it?"
- You've got your singles bar atmosphere of chat rooms, online "affairs," and sometimes even subsequent marriages.
- You've got high crimes and misdemeanors, such as online auction rip-offs and all the icky stuff we don't even want to mention.
- You've got ways to look for a job, order flowers, buy dog food, snoop through public records, look for a place to live, plan your vacation, and purchase just about anything—all with your fanny planted squarely on a chair.
- You've even got virtual funerals. Can't attend a loved one's funeral? Pay your respects by watching the whole thing on your computer screen.

So here's our shtick: Now you've got a virtual party. If you feel like connecting with friends, but you're just too doggone tired to put forth any effort whatsoever to do so, this Bud's for you.

INVITATION

By Phone

"Elaine, I'm rounding up the usual suspects, and we're all going online at seven tonight."

By E-Mail or IM

davekabob: what's better than seeing a buddy online?
cin4lane: dunno, what?

davekabob: seeing ALL your buddies online! LOL! we'll all be online at 7PM, so we'll look for ya!

MENU

Naturally, you'll want to impress your guests with *lavish attention* to both quality and quantity and with how *completely* and *unabashedly* you went over the top with this party. Your menu will show that you *obviously* spared no expense.

Food

- Chateaubriand (Or filet mignon if you feel the chateaubriand is too fussy.)
- *Coquilles St. Jacques*
- Bird's nest potatoes
- *Salade niçoise*
- Light sorbet to cleanse the palate between courses

Beverages

Tonight, only the finest champagne will do—perhaps Dom Perignon?

PROPS AND DÉCOR

- Champagne fountain no less than five tiers high
- Casablanca lilies infusing the room with their heady scent
- Candles placed around a pond, the candlelight reflecting off the speckled skin of the Koi carp
- Harry Winston jewels glittering around the hostess's neck

MUSIC

- Eric Clapton. Live.
- Forty-piece orchestra

Oh, you caught us, didn't you? Yes, our tongues were planted firmly in our cheeks during those last three sections. But we offered those ridiculous suggestions just to make a point: The food, drink, music, and décor can be nonexistent or whatever you want them to be. You can eat frosting out of the can, if that's what you're in the mood for. You don't have to do your hair or even change your clothes. You could be sitting there completely starkers, for all anyone would know.

ENTERTAINMENT

- You will all need to have IM service compatibility in order to "talk" to each other. Using America Online (AOL) as an example, non-AOL members can be compatible with AOL members simply by downloading the AOL Instant Messenger program. Other Internet servers may have this type of service available, but you would need to check with them directly.

- Once you've determined that everyone is ready, willing, and able to participate, away you'll go. You can chat via IM and act for all the world as if you were at a real, live party. Go ahead. Describe your outfit, the menu, the fine champagne. Just don't expect anyone to believe you. Or if you're looking for a little something beyond chat, how about these apples?

    - Create links for each other to look up. With at least twenty squillion web sites at your fingertips, you're sure to come up with a few lollapaloozas to share.

    - Play interactive games online. You'll want to download these games in advance, and some games require special software. Two enormously popular games are Jeopardy! Online, which is a virtual version of the popular television quiz show, and WarBirds, which allows joystick warriors to fly missions over their favorite enemy territory.

    - Tune into a RealPlayer radio station and share the tunes while you play games and chat.

- When you get tired of this party, it's easy to slip out. No excuses, no ten-minutes' worth of trying to get out the door. A quick "gotta go" should take care of it.

> The true beauty of doing anything online is anonymity—which is a double-edged sword, to be sure. Anyone can say anything, and you're not really sure what's true. However, you might as well take advantage of this fact. Only online can every woman be a perfect "10" and every man be a fireman.

182

Come As You Are!

Are you the type who gets itchy fingers when you haven't pulled a good stunt on your friends for a while? If so, we've got a party for the likes of *you!*

You know Mrs. Kravitz, the nosy neighbor on *Bewitched?* In most of her scenes, she's peeking out the windows, and she looks like H-E-double-hockey-sticks, doesn't she? Tattered robe, curlers, face cream. Well, wouldn't your friends look equally amusing if you caught them off guard? That's where the Come As You Are! party comes in. It forces your friends to come to your party at that very moment—no matter what they look like.

Now, we're all for the spirit of *instant,* but even *we* would have a hard time being spontaneous enough to drop everything and go to a party *right this very minute.* So we propose a couple of variations that will get you the same bang for your buck as if the party were held immediately.

Idea Number One: Call your guests the morning of the party and tell them to come to the party that evening, looking exactly how they look that very minute.

Idea Number Two: Give your guests a heads up the night before and tell them you're going to call at *any time* the following day. However they're dressed when the call comes in is how they are to appear at the party. We actually prefer this way of inviting guests. If someone wants to make certain she is absolutely ravishing on Saturday night, well, then she better be that way all Saturday morning and afternoon as well. If someone wants to make sure he's naked, well, that's fine, too.

INVITATION FOR IDEA NUMBER ONE

You'll have to spin a web of deceit as you ensnare your unsuspecting guests. How's this for trickery?

By Phone

"Hi, Jane. What are you doing? ... Don't think me odd, but what are you wearing? ... Exactly, specifically? ... Do you look good? ... Don't make heaven sad by lying!" When she admits she looks horrible, hasn't washed her hair in three days, and is sporting her tooth-bleaching trays, that's when you spring the trap. If she pretends she was just kidding—no, really, she just washed and dried her hair and was experimenting with new lipstick—by all means, tell Jane you are around the corner on your cell phone and are not above making a spot check, if need be.

By E-Mail

What are you wearing? Whatever it is, it's what you'll be wearing tonight at 8:00.

Come tonight as you are right now. I'm going to trust you! Don't make me come over there to check!

Call Charlie 5:00 for details.

INVITATION FOR IDEA NUMBER TWO

If you're going this route, we suggest that prior to your next-day phone calls, find out when your guest takes his shower, mows the lawn, or does some other activity in which you can catch him wearing non-party garb. And by all means, if two guests live together, feel free to invite them separately for maximum effect.

By Phone

"I'm having a come-as-you-are party tomorrow night. I'll call you sometime during the day tomorrow. However I catch you then is how you'll come to the party at eight!"

By E-Mail

I'm having a come-as-you-are party tomorrow night. I'll call you sometime during the day tomorrow. However I catch you then is how you'll come to the party at 8:00!

Don't try any clothing switcheroos after the fact, or the dog gets it!

MENU

This is a make-your-own-taco buffet. All you need to do is set out the ingredients and tableware.

Food

Here are the fixins you'll need to prepare ahead of time:

- Prefried, shaped taco shells: Pop these in the oven as demand decrees. They'll bake up in less than five minutes.
- Cooked seasoned ground beef
- Cooked seasoned cubed chicken
- Grated cheeses (jalapeño, Chihuahua, Cojack)
- Fresh avocados, sliced or in guacamole
- Refried beans softened with a few tablespoons of salsa and sour cream
- Chopped red and green onions
- Chopped black and green olives
- Chopped lettuce
- Chopped tomatoes
- Red and green salsa
- Sour cream
- Our Famous Black Bean Salsa (Just add black beans to your favorite salsa.)
- Variety of tostada chips for dipping
- Dessert: Brush flour tostadas with oil. Bake until crispy, then sprinkle with cinnamon and sugar. It'll take you all of ten minutes to make these.

Beverages

- Margaritas (Natch.)
- Corona or Dos Equis served with lime wedges
- Soda
- Flavored essence water
- Cinnamon coffee

- Chocolate coffee: Set a square of Hershey's milk chocolate in a coffee cup. Fill the cup halfway with strong black coffee. Fill the rest with hot cream.

PROPS AND DÉCOR

Make sure you have plenty of light. Nobody should be able to hide in the shadows tonight—no matter what they look like.

MUSIC

- When your guests first arrive, get things going with something spicy and feel-good, like Tejano music. Even though they might look hideous and/or hilarious, you'll still want them to have a good time. Here are a few Tejano artists to sample:
  - Ruben Ramos
  - Johnny Hernandez
  - Josefa
  - La Movida
  - Selena
  - Texas Tornados
  - Los Lobos
  - The Mavericks
- After a short time, let the party and the guests take it from there. They may want to dance to their favorites, start singing, or do who knows what. Just go with the flow and keep it lively.

ENTERTAINMENT

- Well, depending on how your guests show up, their appearance may provide more entertainment than you bargained for. But overall, this is your basic mix-and-mingle party, and it's not necessary to provide any organized entertainment.
- If you do feel in the mood for a game, here's a suggestion: Everyone will no doubt discuss where they were when they received the invitation to the party.

Spin that discussion into a game of "Where Were You When...?" Have each guest answer one question drawn out of a bowl or have all guests answer one question in a round robin. Certainly, the questions will depend upon your guests' ages and personalities. Take a peek at our list and go from there.

Where were you when...

- the Beatles first came to America?
- you received your first kiss?
- the Berlin Wall came down?
- you experienced your most embarrassing moment?
- Neil Armstrong walked on the moon?
- you knew you had arrived?
- Charles and Diana were married?
- you realized no one's got it all figured out?
- you were the happiest?
- you ran into your former boy- or girlfriend?

> About that one guest who showed up dressed to the nines, coifed, made-up, and insisting with her magnolia-accented, sweet-as-tupelo-honey protestations: "No, really. Ah *swear* Ah *always* look lahk this at eight on a Saturday mornin'!" Well, you can take care of her the *next* time you get itchy fingers.

Hootenanny

As reluctant as Andy Griffith was to see the Darlings camped out on his front porch in Mayberry, their cries of "Sheriff, play one for us, will ya?" invariably sent him scurrying inside after his guitar.

A hootenanny is good, clean fun. You'd be surprised how easily people get caught up in an old-fashioned sing-along. We know because we've seen it: "Kumbaya," that old sappy relic of the sixties, always starts with uproarious laughter and ridicule, then, without fail, someone always ends up *farklempt* before it's over.

Other people get so caught up in the magic of a hootenanny that they sing right along, even when they don't know the lyrics. We wish you could've been there when we sang Neil Diamond's "Forever in Blue Jeans" at our hootenanny. There was Mitch, singing along at the top of his lungs, "I'd rather be *Reverend Blue Jeans.*" And there, too, was Cindy. Even though she was the biggest Beatle fan that Springfield, Missouri, ever saw, she still managed to twist the words of "I'm a Loser" from "is it for her or myself that I cry" to "is it for *hair on myself* that I cry."

A word of caution here, folks: Do refer to this party as a "hootenanny." Don't call it a "sing-along," or no one will come because they'll be afraid. Afraid that you'll fill them with the "Michael, Row the Boat Ashore"-ishness that sing-alongs invariably promote. They'll think you're pushing a *Let's save the world!* type of thing, when all you'll really want them to do is roast some wieners and sing some songs.

INVITATION

By Phone

(Sing to the tune of "Abraham, Martin, and John.")

"Anybody heeeeere seen my old friend David? Can you tell me where he's gone?" After David laughs, simply invite him over for a hootenanny and campfire goodies.

By E-Mail

(Sing to the tune of "Abraham, Martin, and John.")

Anybody heeeeere seen my old friend Julie? Can you tell me where she's gone?

Can you join us tonight for a hootenanny and campfire goodies? Call me!

MENU

We said campfire goodies, and we mean campfire goodies! We see this as an outdoor party, so if you can get hold of one of those portable fireplaces, we highly recommend going that route. If you'll be indoors and have a real fireplace, that would work, too. Use plastic picnicware or quality paper plates.

Food

- Hot dogs roasted on a stick: It's been said time and time again. There's nothing more fun than holding your wiener over an open flame.
- A basket full of hot dog buns, ketchup, mustard, and relish
- Cold-cut sandwiches
- Marshmallows: Roast 'em over the fire till they're all brown and gooey.
- Baked beans served in coffee mugs
- Cold navy bean salad with olive oil, vinegar, and chopped red and green peppers
- Chips and dips
- S'mores (Roast the marshmallows as instructed above.)
- Brownie ice-cream sammiches: Cut thin brownies into squares and sandwich vanilla ice cream between pairs of them.

Beverages

- Beer
- Pale ale
- Hardened apple or lemonade cider
- Soda
- Flavored water

PROPS AND DÉCOR

- Boom box or an easily portable sound system
- Extensive collection of tapes and CDs
- "Sit-upons," such as pillows and sleeping bags
- Citronella candles
- Bug spray

MUSIC AND ENTERTAINMENT

- If you're fortunate enough to know someone who plays guitar, by all means, ask her to strum for you. If that's the case, then it's practically mandatory that you make copies of the lyrics. When there's a CD to sing along with, the artist will always carry the day. But when it's just a guitar and *you*—and you can't remember all the words—the song will die right there on the vine.
- When it comes to choosing music, here are a few classic artists that might be fun to sing along with:
  - Folk artists: The workhorses of the hootenanny.
    - Pete Seeger
    - Peter, Paul and Mary
    - Woody and Arlo Guthrie
    - Bob Dylan
    - The Limeliters
  - Rock artists
    - Neil Young
    - America
    - Simon and Garfunkel
    - The Everly Brothers
    - The Beach Boys
- If all else fails, try the song that's in a class by itself: "My Ding-a-Ling" by Chuck Berry.

> At a hootenanny, 98 percent of the time we want other people to hear us singing. But that 2 percent of the time when we can't hit a note, our chins drop, we look the other way, we smile, we nod along to the music. Don't believe us? Try singing along with the Bee Gees.

Musings

The Antidote

Whether you've ever been diagnosed with clinical depression or not, you may want to flag this page. Why, you ask? Because one day it may save your life from a secret killer. A killer so silent and so insidious that some would deny its power. *Fools!*

The killer goes by many names, but here in the Midwest, we call it what it is: Unrelenting Gray Weather (UGW). Yes, friends, we're talking about the UGW that knows no shame. When this same UGW has the unmitigated gall to rear its ugly head, it takes twice the patience of Job not to declare an all-out abort of the entire day. How is it that UGW can take relatively happy, well-adjusted, contributing members of society and reduce them to bitter believers in *What the hell—ya live alone, ya die alone*?

It's time to take action and beat this demon at its own game! This he- or she-devil—we know not which (or perhaps there are *two!*)—wants to keep you inside, behind doors. "Fine," we say, "then it's behind doors we'll stay. *But on our own terms!*"

After enduring a long spell of UGW, we are driven to these lengths: To either throw in the towel entirely or declare an entire day dedicated to trivia games. We prefer the latter. It's time to rise up and shed that sallow pallor of defeat and replace it with the rosy glow of triumph!

At your UGW Antidote party, the beer will flow freely, the dice and the good times will roll, and the name UGW will not be uttered. May we suggest you even go so far as to pull the shades. Then It can't even see you.

INVITATION

By Phone

YOU: Good morning on this lovely day.
THEY: Yeah, right. Another day of this crap and you'll have to have me committed.

YOU: No, really, we're in luck! If it were nice out, we'd never stay inside to play trivia games all afternoon!

By E-Mail

We're in luck! The weather forecast for the entire weekend is for gray skies and all-around crappy weather!

If that weren't the case, we'd never get the gang together for trivia games this afternoon! Can you join us? Call Grace for details.

MENU

Because it's so rotten outside, you may as well go ahead and make a nice meal. After all, what else better do you have to do? This is an easy menu, so preparing it won't make your mood any worse than it already is. Instead, it will go a long way toward taking the gloom out of the day.

Food

- Marinated and broiled chicken breasts: Make up several plastic zip bags of marinade, using a different marinade in each bag, such as southwestern, zesty herb, or oriental. Marinate two or three breasts in each bag for an hour. Broil (since it's not bloody likely you'll be out by the grill today), then slice into medallions. Serve either warm or at room temperature. Have guests choose among the cuts.
- Grecian fries: Slice potatoes lengthwise into 6 equal parts. Spray with olive oil and season with salt, pepper, oregano, basil, and Parmesan. Bake at 400°F for approximately 40 minutes, or until tender and brown.
- Tossed salad: Start with finely chopped lettuce. Add black olives, feta, and cucumber that's been seeded then chopped. Toss with a good quality olive oil and red-wine vinegar. Season with salt, oregano, and coarsely ground pepper.
- Pita bread: Onion pita is great, if you can find that. Warm, cut into halves, and serve in a basket covered with a cloth napkin. Guests can tuck the sliced chicken and greens into the pita halves, if they choose. Have extra salad dressing on hand.
- Yogurt dip for the pitas: Mix plain yogurt with cumin, crushed garlic, salt, and lemon.

- Baked apples with cinnamon, nutmeg, brown sugar, and maple syrup: You deserve every last bite of gooiness on a day like today, so serve them in small bowls with spoons. If you've recently been to confession, serve with French vanilla ice cream.

Beverages

- Beer
- Wine: Offer your favorites along with a few nonalcoholic selections.
- Ice water
- Iced coffee
- Hot coffee with dessert

PROPS AND DÉCOR

The lighting is going to be an issue here. Here it is, the middle of the doggone day, and it's nearly nighttime dark outside. You'll probably need lamps with low-watt bulbs and maybe a few candles around. Not too many candles, however, or the party could take on the look of a wake. And that's not going to do anyone any good.

MUSIC

Better keep that music extra lively today. Mix it up: jazz, Latin, and oldies rock. May we offer a few suggestions?

- Bruce Springsteen
- Harry Belafonte
- The Beach Boys
- Boz Scaggs
- Barbara Streisand
- Ethel Merman
- Judy Garland
- The Eagles
- Bee Gees
- Bob Marley
- Mel Tormé
- Lena Horne singing—what else?
  —"Stormy Weather"

ENTERTAINMENT

- There are so many trivia games on the market these days, if you don't already have one, you'll find them very easy to come by. Invite your friends to bring their own trivia games as well. We've listed just the tip of the iceberg when it comes to trivia games. We think these should keep you busy till the sun comes out again.
    - Trivial Pursuit (There are at least ten different editions.)
    - The *I Love Lucy* Trivia Game
    - The All Canadian Trivia Board Game (English and French versions available)
    - Go For Launch!: Space Encyclopedia Board Game
    - Reel Schpeel: The Movie and Celebrity Game
    - Auction America: The Trivia Game for Any Collector
    - For the Record: Rock & Roll Trivia Game
    - Bible Trivia
    - Titanic Trivia Game
    - *The Wizard of Oz* Trivia Game
    - *The Andy Griffith Show* Trivia Game
    - Jeopardy!

- There are as many kinds of players as there are trivia games. Some people take forever to answer. When we play trivia games, we always use a stopwatch or an egg timer to time the responses; otherwise, some players think they are entitled to an hour per answer. Other players can barely stay in their seats, as though levitating their hind ends will somehow ensure that their answer is correct! And *my*, some players take things way too seriously. With one wrong answer, Mr. Smartypants morphs into Mr. Poutypants right before your very eyes.

> Playing trivia games automatically ensures that there will be a roller coaster of energy whizzing through the room, so just never you mind about that stupid old UGW! Come to think of it, once you get the vibes humming with your trivia party, go ahead and pull those window shades back up and thumb your nose right in the face of UGW. Let It see how much fun you're having. See how It likes *that*.

195

Sunday Morning

On Sunday morning, we all want to be comfortable. We want fresh orange juice and steamy coffee. We want bagels, croissants, and juicy red strawberries. We want to linger in our tattered robes or comfy sweats.

We want to gather with our friends. We want to enjoy one another's company yet spread out with the *Sunday Times* or *Newsweek*. All in all, we want to be so darn comfortable with where we are and who we are that we don't have to force conversation. We just want to *be*.

This party lets you spend a few peaceful, laid-back hours with your friends and neighbors. It brings about a cozy feeling of intimacy and down-home comfort.

It's easy—easy like Sunday morning.

INVITATION

Maybe when you see that "red sky at night," the omen will move you to call up a few friends and enjoy what promises to be a lovely morning. We happen to think guests will be happier if you invite them Saturday evening rather than wake them up bright and early Sunday morning. An e-mail invitation may not be read late at night or early in the morning, so we won't include one here. Also note that your guests will most likely live in your neighborhood and may come over in their bathrobes. How lovely would that be? At any rate, it's pretty certain that guests won't come from out of town for this one.

By Phone

"Lee, it's Sherry. Tomorrow's supposed to be gorgeous, so how about coming over at nine? We're going to have some wonderful things for breakfast, and we'll even pick up the morning newspapers for you."

MENU

Make absolutely certain that the livin' is easy at this party. The menu we've created allows you to pick up everything at the bakery or grocery store the night before and then present it as a buffet.

Food

- Croissants
- Scones
- Bagels, such as cinnamon, blueberry, onion, and plain
- Fruit breads, such as banana, orange date, cranberry, and lemon
- Finger fruits, such as strawberries, grapes, and Bing cherries (Provide little dishes for the pits and stems.)
- Apple slices drizzled with lime juice
- Cream cheese
- Butter whipped or cut into pats
- Sour cream for dipping fruit: Use plain sour cream or mix sour cream with brown sugar, mashed ripe banana, cinnamon, and vanilla.

Beverages

- Bottomless pot of coffee: Leaded or unleaded, whichever most of your guests prefer.
- Tea
- Juice: Dole makes wonderful blended juices, such as Strawberry Orange Banana and Pineapple Orange.
- Cranberry juice and sparkling water
- Mimosas

PROPS AND DÉCOR

- Being the fair maidens of summer that we are, we see this as a midsummer party, when the sun is out early and it's already warm at nine in the morning. If you have a patio or any space outdoors, use your lawn furniture, carry tables and chairs outside, or use the picnic table.

- We're speaking strictly for ourselves here, but we would be hard-pressed to host this party if there was any kind of a nip in the air. However, you may be the type of person who loves morning darkness and sees Sunday morning as an opportunity to use the fireplace. That will work, too, "if you like that sort of thing," as one of our grandmothers used to say.

MUSIC

Keep it mellow. We'd want the kind of music you might hear through someone's screen door on a sleepy, dusty day—the kind of music they play on the *real old* oldies station. Or how about these ideas:

- Light jazz
- Classical
- New Age
- *Sounds of Nature* recordings
- Anything by Andrea Bocelli

ENTERTAINMENT

- Perhaps guests will just want to bury their noses in the morning papers. We imagine both monthly periodicals and dailies spread out for guests to peruse. You'll need to make a quick run in the morning to a newsstand. Here's a sampling of what your guests might enjoy:
  - Your hometown daily
  - An out-of-town daily
  - *International Herald Tribune*
  - *London Times*
  - *New York Times*
  - *Wall Street Journal*
  - *Time*
  - *Newsweek*
  - A variety of monthly mags
- Some guests may wish to merely sit and chat. If your friends tend to be bookish—or even if they don't—you may enjoy exchanging views on what you're reading.
- Other guests may want to be alone with their thoughts, relaxing in the peace of the morning and the company of others.

> This gathering reminds us of a most affable fellow: the late, great Charles Kuralt. On his Sunday morning television show, he presented segments at a peaceful pace, and he made us feel the way we imagined we were supposed to feel on a Sunday morning. Though Charles Kuralt is gone, we hope this party brings that same air of comfort and relaxation to your Sunday morning.

Fireside Chats

Well, glory hallelujah, that fireplace you so long dreamed of has at last been installed. Now you need to wait for the perfect time to have friends over to enjoy it with you! You know, when the snow is just fluffy enough or the autumn leaves are just russet enough or the sounds of an April night are just hypnotic enough...

Oh, snap out of it, would you? The time is *now*, friend! You need to *carpe* this very *diem* and use that fireplace to introduce your friends to a different sort of a gathering.

If you ever figure out what is so relaxing about the glow of a fire, let us know, because we want to bottle it, sell it, and retire to Tahiti. Logically, glow-induced relaxation is followed by glow-induced contemplation, and we think you should take full advantage of this very fact. The glow of that fire will create the perfect backdrop for some interesting chats with your friends. Quite frankly, if Fireside Chats worked for Franklin D. Roosevelt, chances are they'll work for you, too!

INVITATION

By Phone

"Mike, Tom and I are enjoying a fire and setting out sandwiches. Can you join us at seven tonight?"

By E-Mail

Join us in front of the fire tonight at 7:00. Come for dinner. Fireside Chats included.

Call Tom by 5:00.

MENU

In front of the fireplace, set out low coffee tables covered with tablecloths and set with serviceware and linen napkins. Eating and chatting can then take place simultaneously.

Food

- *Pepperoncini* beef sandwiches: Early in the day, place a beef roast in the slow cooker. Add a jar of pepperoncini (including the juice but minus the stems). Allow this to cook all day. When it's done, shred the meat. Return it to the cooker till serving time. Using a slotted ladle, serve on crispy French rolls. These sandwiches need absolutely no condiments; they are perfect by themselves.
- Potato chips
- Cole slaw: There's the "squeaky kind," and the "creamy kind." We found the creamy version to be more complementary to these sandwiches.
- Fruit cobblers: Peach, blueberry, apple, cherry—whatever fruit you use, double that delicious topping!
- Bowls of fresh fruit

Beverages

- Coffee
- Tea
- Sherry: Offer different types of sherry: cream, dry, or sweet. Serve straight or on the rocks with a lemon twist. Keep the bottles in an ice bucket within easy reach.

PROPS AND DÉCOR

- Have pillows, pillows, and more pillows stacked in a heap so your guests can take what they'll need to get comfy.
- If you don't have a fireplace, you can still achieve the same ambiance with candles. You'll need about two dozen placed at different heights in one general area.
- If guests will be arriving after dark, how about lighting the path to your door? This can be easily done with votive candles in Mason jars.

MUSIC

Choose music that will subtly fill the background but won't distract your guests. At our Fireside Chats party, we played gentle, soothing Asian music. We also include a few other selections:

- *Beat the Border* by Geoffrey Oryema
- *Fold Your Hands Child...* by Belle and Sebastian
- *A Journey into Ambient Groove 4*
- *Instrumental Moods*
- Your favorite classical recordings

ENTERTAINMENT

- Our vision of Fireside Chats is that you will create a cove in which you and your friends can discuss values, beliefs, and ethics. The point is not to reach unilateral agreement, but to learn about one another and yourselves. What's great about these kinds of topics is that there are no right or wrong answers.

- There's a wonderful little paperback we recommend you pick up. It was a *New York Times* bestseller, in fact, so lots of people agree with us. It's *The Book of Questions* (Workman Publishing Company, 1987) by Gregory Stock, Ph.D. Besides being a perfect companion to this party, the book is also great for long car trips. Here are some questions from the book:

  - "Would you be willing to give up sex for one year if you knew it would give you a much deeper sense of peace than you have now?"
  - "What things are too personal to discuss with others?"
  - "Would you rather be happy yet slow-witted and unimaginative, or unhappy yet bright and creative? For example, would you rather live the life of a brilliant yet tortured artist, such as Vincent van Gogh, or that of a happy but carefree soul who is a bit simple-minded?"

> A fireplace provides the perfect venue for you to learn more about your friends and yourself. The glow of the fire might even inspire you to (gasp!) change your opinion about something! Aren't you glad you didn't wait for that perfect day when the autumn leaves were just russet enough to decide to throw this party?

The Equinox, the Solstice, and the Sky

When we start talking about the enormity of the universe, the discussions become positively mind-blowing. We personally feel creeped out, because neither of us is comfortable with the universe being either finite or infinite. The theory of it being *infinite* completely leaves us at loose ends, while the idea of it being *finite* gets us feeling boxed in to the point where it becomes difficult to breathe!

In order to keep ourselves from feeling too edgy, we thought we'd take a poll and find out how others felt about this topic. It was a great excuse to have a party.

We didn't choose the night we hosted this party—*it* chose *us*. It was one of those rare nights: warm weather, clear skies, full moon, no mosquitoes. We were joined by friends from the neighborhood, who, as it turned out, had been looking for some way to celebrate such a glorious night. We laid back on blankets, looked at the sky, talked about what we thought might be up there, and expressed how it made us feel.

Whether you choose to examine the stars or the theories that explain them, there's enough of both to keep you busy for a few light-years.

INVITATION

By Phone

"Hello, Shirley? It's written in the stars that you'll come to my house tonight at eight—no, no wait! My celestial vibrations are saying 'nine.' We want you to join us for a sky show!"

By E-Mail

When the Moon is in the seventh house
And Jupiter aligns with Mars...

You'll be at my house, searching the sky for all of them! Can you join us tonight at 9:00 for a night of celestial musings?

Call Claire before 5:00.

MENU

Your guests will attend the best show in town tonight, so why not make the munchies fall in line with what you might find at the movies? Have paper napkins and wet wipes available.

Food

- Popcorn: Get one of those tins with three flavors of popcorn and separate the flavors into individual brown lunch bags. Let everybody choose a bag.
- Licorice whips
- M&M's
- Milk Duds
- Raisinets
- York peppermint patties
- Milky Way candy bars
- Gummi bears
- Good & Plenty, Atomic FireBalls, Lemonheads, and other candy that's good only till you've sucked off the coating
- Cashews
- Honey-roasted peanuts
- Pistachios
- Nonpareils: Neither of us voted for these, but one of our husbands wanted them included. Well, they *do* look like little dark skies filled with stars, so we decided to give the baby his bottle.

Beverages

- Chardonnay: It's great with sweets!
- Sparkling water
- Bottled mineral water
- Soda

PROPS AND DÉCOR

Can you imagine the wonderment of having this party when a meteor shower is scheduled for your area? Or a lunar eclipse? But such celestial displays are rare, so you and your guests will most likely lie back and enjoy the usual midsummer night's sky. Here are some items that will help you do just that:

- Telescope: If you don't own one, can you beg, borrow, or rent one?
- Binoculars: No, you won't see into the next galaxy with these, but you'll see formations on the moon much more clearly.
- Lawn chairs, sleeping bags, blankets, or anything that allows guests to lie on their backs and be comfortable
- Bug spray and citronella candles (Keep the candles far enough away so the light does not interfere with the stargazing.)
- Books on astronomy, constellations, and astrology

MUSIC

We don't recommend you listen to music while you're stargazing. It would be insulting to interrupt those chirping crickets. But when you decide to come inside, here are a few ideas:

- *The Planets* composed by Gustav Holst
- And here it gets hokey... Play a few songs from this list or find some "celestial" songs from your own collection.
    - "Moon River" by Andy Williams
    - "Fly Me to the Moon" by Frank Sinatra
    - "Everybody Is a Star" by Sly and the Family Stone
    - "Moon over Miami" by Eddy Duchin

- "The Warmth of the Sun" by The Beach Boys
- "Sunday Will Never Be the Same" by Spanky and Our Gang (Get it?)
- "Moondance" by Van Morrison
- "Sunny" by Dusty Springfield
- "House of the Rising Sun" by The Animals
- "Aquarius" by The 5th Dimension

ENTERTAINMENT

- If you live near a planetarium, call to find out what's playing that night in the sky. (Are any meteors, planets, and so on visible?)

- Many astronomy web sites and books provide constellation guides. First pick out the constellations you know (the extent for us is the Big and Little Dippers), and then see if you can't locate any others listed in your constellation guide. You'll no doubt hear cries of "I don't see a bear!" but don't be discouraged. Even if you never pick out a single constellation, you will still enjoy the peaceful, easy feeling with a billion stars all around.

- When people get tired of stargazing, either move inside or stay put, but steer the party in a different direction. Introduce the topic of astronomy's less-revered cousin, astrology. Although astrology has many believers, it has equally as many skeptics who feel the entire business doesn't stand up to scrutiny. Maybe read that day's horoscopes from your daily paper. Whichever group your guests side with, it'll be an interesting topic to debate.

- You could also introduce the whole extraterrestrial debate. You could discuss that one till the stars disappear in the morning light.

> Researching this party placed us in the presence of the writings and teachings of a man whose name we are not worthy to even utter out loud, so we'll just whisper it: *Stephen Hawking*. If the universe makes you feel insignificant, try reading some of *his* stuff! Let's just say this party touches on some theories of cosmology that *Stephen Hawking* probably thought of at one time, too. The difference being that he would have hosted this party when he was four. But we, like the universe, have to start *somewhere*.

Beethoven, Books, and Bull

We never fail to wonder what's with that I-beam in front of the civic center. And you know, we tried reading *The Old Man and the Sea.* Not only did the fish escape, but for us so did the whole point of the story.

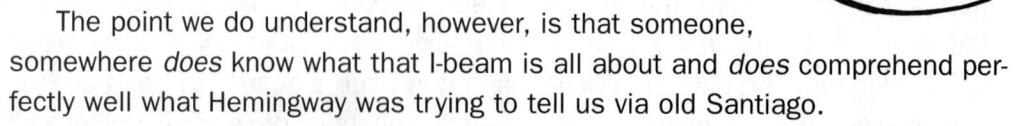

The point we do understand, however, is that someone, somewhere *does* know what that I-beam is all about and *does* comprehend perfectly well what Hemingway was trying to tell us via old Santiago.

We think it's a good idea to look at life from different perspectives once in a while, and art and philosophy are stimulating outlets through which to do that. One night, we gathered a group of friends who seemed to have an opinion on everything. We also gathered material that was ripe for discussion: art books, different types of music, philosophy books, and more. We wanted to enlighten one another. Just because we didn't "get" the I-beam didn't mean there wasn't something to "get."

You, too, can have a night of lively and fun discussions about topics you didn't think you knew enough about to discuss. You might be surprised what you and your friends can teach one another.

INVITATION

By Phone

YOU: Andrew, you know what I was thinking?
THEY: What was that?
YOU: Our opinions about art and philosophy never seem to get enough airtime. I thought we could get together tonight and let them breathe. Are you available at seven? We'll have drinks and snacks.

By E-Mail

Our opinions about art and philosophy never seem to get enough airtime. I thought we could get together tonight and let them breathe.

Join us tonight at 7:00. Bring an appetite for both food and discussion.

Call Meg before 5:00.

MENU

Tonight might be the time to experiment with your menu. Since people are coming with their minds wide open, ready to hear varying opinions and new ideas, they may feel more avant-garde nibbling at something they may not normally eat. But don't worry; this experimental menu can be prepared in the time it takes to get to a deli or restaurant and back. Set up a buffet and let guests help themselves.

Food

- Pâtés served with French bread or crackers
- Hummus with pita
- Thinly sliced lox with lemon, coarsely ground black pepper, and green onions and served with cream cheese and mini bagels
- Tabbouleh
- Pot stickers
- Cold Thai beef salad
- Hot-and-sour soup

Beverages

- Martinis with bleu-cheese-stuffed olives
- White French table wine
- Sparkling mineral water
- Sparkling flavored-essence water
- Flavored coffee: Sure, there are other flavored coffees out there, but this goes beyond mixing a packet of powder and boiling water. This is dessert in a

cup. You can even top it with a dollop of heavy whipped cream or vanilla ice cream. Brew strong black coffee and add the following:

- Caramel or butterscotch ice-cream topping
- Miniature York peppermint patties
- Raspberry ice-cream topping and chocolate syrup
- Chocolate-covered cherry cordials
- Maple syrup
- Fun-size candy bars, such as Reese's Peanut Butter Cups, Milky Way, 3 Musketeers, and Snickers
- Fruit pie fillings

PROPS AND DÉCOR

- Go to the library ahead of time and get a variety of books that include topics such as art, music, literature, and philosophy.
- Also find two or three library books that have an old, scholarly look. Stack them askew on the buffet table. Arranged in this fashion, you can place small, interesting items—such as candles on saucers, small glasses filled with flowers, and pottery pieces—on the books.

MUSIC

No need to buy a bunch of new CDs or tapes. Just hit the library and pick out music from genres you might not normally listen to. Need ideas?

- Classical
- Opera
- Jazz
- Spirituals
- World music
- Bluegrass
- Rap

ENTERTAINMENT

Grab those martinis and hunker down somewhere comfy. Let your discussion take you wherever it leads. Here's how to get started:

- An icebreaker is always a welcome idea. When we hosted this party, we handed Lane a book and announced in a big-busted, garden-club voice: "And nooooow, Lane will read—in its original Greek—Homer's *Iliad*." After the initial *tee hees*, our guests were comfortable and ready to tackle a night of cerebral musings.
- Flip through the library books and comment on anything interesting. Maybe you'll come upon a critical essay on Beethoven's Symphony no. 5. It would be great to read from the essay while you listen to the piece. Or maybe you'll come upon a photograph of Picasso's *Nude Woman*. It will easily spur the discussion of the different ways art expresses reality.
- You may want to put the books aside and start your own lively discussions. Here are a couple of sample questions you might want to pose:
  - Socrates once said people make choices based on their own convenience. (We have said the exact same thing. But do you see *our* names anywhere in the history books? No, because he got it in print first, and that's the only reason.) Do you agree with Socrates (and us)?
  - Is all art economy driven? (Naturally, this does not apply to us or to our book.)
  - *If there's only room for one person in the lifeboat, I'm taking it.* Do you agree or disagree? (And if you agree, are you ashamed?)

> Revolving the conversations around artists and philosophers (instead of presidents and popes) ensures that your party will not likely turn into the usual Friday Night Fight, since neither the state of the union nor mortal souls are at stake.

AFTERTHOUGHTS

The very foundation of civilization as we know it may well be the fine art of socialization. Throughout history, however, our ancestors did not always do well when it came to entertaining. There have been plenty of events that had the earmarks of good parties—be they instant or long-planned—yet they somehow fell short.

Take the Creation, for starters. The Garden of Eden had perfect weather, flowers, fresh fruit, a guy, and a gal. A talking serpent added interest and diversity. But Adam and Eve messed things up, and finally God flashed the lights and said, "Goodnight, everybody."

There's also the Ostrogoths and Visigoths' invasions. It wasn't enough that they were unwanted guests who had invited themselves to the Roman Empire's parties. No, they had to pillage and plunder to boot!

Then we hearken back to Caligula's rule over ancient Rome. He sent party antics to a new low. After an evening of lewd, crude behavior, it's hard to believe guests were even able to face one another for a "next time" (see "Stone of Shame" on page 176).

And how about that Boston Tea Party? *Harumph*, we say! Anything but a party, that one!

Of course, none of the players in these events were privy to the book you're now holding in your hot little hands. If they could have read fifty of the most fun, quick, and easy parties known to humankind—as you have—they may not have strayed from the path of entertainment decorum.

We hope that after reading this book, you've come to the conclusion we hoped you would come to: Entertaining isn't really so hard. Keep a spirit of playfulness and a sense of humor, and you're more than halfway there. After all, the future of humankind isn't at stake. Your ambition is always to have fun. Bear that in mind, and all your entertaining endeavors should be rip-snortin' successes.

INDEX

Activities. *See* Entertainment
Antidote theme, 192–95
Any Given Sunday theme, 77–80
Art appreciation
  Beethoven, books, and bull theme, 206–09
Astrology, 34, 205
Astronomy
  equinox, the solstice, and the sky theme, 202–05

Bad weather
  antidote theme, 192–95
Baked goods, 100
Bakery Dinner theme, 99–102
Beethoven, Books, and Bull theme, 206–09
Beverages
  antidote theme, 194
  any given Sunday theme, 79
  bakery dinner theme, 101
  Beethoven, books, and bull theme, 207–08
  blue plate special theme, 92
  Bond. James Bond. theme, 37
  Chinatown theme, 116
  come as you are theme, 186
  commune dinner theme, 84
  cookbook pass-around theme, 108
  divide and conquer theme, 113
  done yer duty theme, 88
  equinox, the solstice, and the sky theme, 204
  fireside chats theme, 200
  Frank Sinatra's real swingin' affair theme, 14–15
  fright fest theme, 4
  Hans Brinker, or the silver skates theme, 70
  happy trails to you! theme, 174
  Havana! theme, 29
  hide-and-seek in the dark and on the floor theme, 58
  hootenanny theme, 189
  hot wax night theme, 158
  hubristic tour theme, 128–29
  it's a marvelous night for a moondance theme, 11
  magical mystery party theme, 32
  Marrakesh express theme, 42
  Munich meets Milwaukee theme, 133–34
  new blood theme, 163
  Noel Coward's brief encounter theme, 24
  okay, but not at my house theme, 171
  outdoor summer games for big kids theme, 53
  pajama game theme, 146
  pool (pocket) theme, 66
  pool (swimming) theme, 62
  progressive leaf raking theme, 126
  radio days theme, 166–67
  ragin' Cajun theme, 105
  señora, que quiere? theme, 46, 47, 49
  shangri-la-de-da (de da) theme, 96–97
  showtime! theme, 154
  story weaver theme, 141
  strangers theme, 7–8
  summer of love theme, 19
  Sunday morning theme, 197
  Venus flytrap theme, 151
  vice-free party theme, 177
  virtual party theme, 181
  we're rollin'! theme, 75
  whine and cheese theme, 138
  wild abandon theme, 121–22
Blue Plate Special theme, 90–93
Bond. James Bond. theme, 35–39
Breakfast diner
  blue plate special theme, 90–93
Breakfast parties
  blue plate special theme, 90–93
  Sunday morning theme, 196–98

Casino, 38–39
Cerebral discussions
  Beethoven, books, and bull theme, 206–09
  equinox, the solstice, and the sky theme, 202–05
  fireside chats theme, 199–201
Children, parties with
  progressive leaf raking theme, 124–26
  vice-free party theme, 176–79
Chinatown theme, 115–18
Cocktail parties
  Bond. James Bond. theme, 35–39
  Frank Sinatra's real swingin' affair theme, 13–16
  pool (swimming) theme, 60–63
  shangri-la-de-da (de da) theme, 94–98
  strangers theme, 6–9
Come as You Are theme, 183–87
Commune Dinner theme, 82–85
Complaining, 136–39
Cookbook Pass-Around theme, 107–10
Coward, Noel, 22
Cuba, 27

Décor. *See* Props and décor
Dinner parties
  bakery dinner theme, 99–102
  Chinatown theme, 115–18
  commune dinner theme, 82–85
  cookbook pass-around theme, 107–10
  divide and conquer theme, 111–14
  done yer duty theme, 86–89
  Frank Sinatra's real swingin' affair theme, 13–14
  Havana! theme, 27–30
  magical mystery party theme, 31–34
  Noel Coward's brief encounter theme, 22–26
  okay, but not at my house! theme, 169–70
  pool (swimming) theme, 60–63
  pool (pocket) theme, 64–67
  radio days theme, 165–68
  ragin' Cajun theme, 103–06
  story weaver theme, 140–43
  Venus flytrap theme, 148–52
Done Yer Duty theme, 86–89

211

Eastern European food, 32
Elegant parties
 Beethoven, books, and bull theme, 206–09
 Bond. James Bond. theme, 35–39
 divide and conquer theme, 111–14
 Frank Sinatra's real swingin' affair theme, 13–14
 Marrakesh express theme, 40–43
 Noel Coward's brief encounter theme, 22–26
 pool (swimming) theme, 60–63
 radio days theme, 165–68
 ragin' Cajun theme, 103–06
 strangers theme, 6–9
English garden party
 Noel Coward's brief encounter theme, 22–26
Entertainment
 antidote theme, 195
 any given Sunday theme, 79–80
 bakery dinner theme, 101–02
 Beethoven, books, and bull theme, 208–09
 blue plate special theme, 93
 Bond. James Bond. theme, 38–39
 Chinatown theme, 117–18
 come as you are theme, 186–87
 commune dinner theme, 85
 cookbook pass-around theme, 109–10
 divide and conquer theme, 114
 done yer duty theme, 89
 equinox, the solstice, and the sky theme, 205
 fireside chats theme, 201
 Frank Sinatra's real swingin' affair theme, 16
 fright fest theme, 4–5
 Hans Brinker, or the silver skates theme, 71–72
 happy trails to you! theme, 175
 Havana! theme, 30
 hide-and-seek in the dark and on the floor theme, 59
 hootenanny theme, 190
 hot wax night theme, 160
 hubristic tour theme, 129–30
 it's a marvelous night for a moondance theme, 12

magical mystery party theme, 33–34
Marrakesh express theme, 43
Munich meets Milwaukee theme, 134–35
new blood theme, 163–64
Noel Coward's brief encounter theme, 26
okay, but not at my house theme, 172
outdoor summer games for big kids theme, 54–56
pajama game theme, 147
pool (pocket) theme, 67
pool (swimming) theme, 63
progressive leaf raking theme, 126
radio days theme, 167–68
ragin' Cajun theme, 106
señora, que quiere? theme, 46–47, 48, 49
shangri-la-de-da (de da) theme, 98
showtime! theme, 155–56
story weaver theme, 142–43
strangers theme, 9
summer of love theme, 21
Sunday morning theme, 198
Venus flytrap theme, 152
vice-free party theme, 179
virtual party theme, 182
we're rollin'! theme, 75–76
whine and cheese theme, 138–39
wild abandon theme, 122–23
Equinox, the Solstice, and the Sky theme, 202–05
Exotic atmosphere
 Havana! theme, 27–30
 Marrakesh express theme, 40–43
 pool (swimming) theme, 60–63
 ragin' Cajun theme, 103–06

Fifties parties
 Havana! theme, 27–30
 hot wax night theme, 157–60
Fire, parties by a
 fireside chats theme, 199–201
 hootenanny theme, 188–90
Fireside Chats theme, 199–201
Food
 antidote theme, 193–94
 any given Sunday theme, 78–79
 bakery dinner theme, 100–01

Beethoven, books, and bull theme, 207
blue plate special theme, 91–92
Bond. James Bond. theme, 36
Chinatown theme, 116
come as you are theme, 185
commune dinner theme, 83–84
cookbook pass-around theme, 108
divide and conquer theme, 112–13
done yer duty theme, 87–88
equinox, the solstice, and the sky theme, 203
fireside chats theme, 200
Frank Sinatra's real swingin' affair theme, 14
fright fest theme, 3
Hans Brinker, or the silver skates theme, 70
happy trails to you! theme, 174
Havana! theme, 28
hide-and-seek in the dark and on the floor theme, 58
hootenanny theme, 189
hot wax night theme, 158
hubristic tour theme, 128
it's a marvelous night for a moondance theme, 11
magical mystery party theme, 32
Marrakesh express theme, 41–42
Munich meets Milwaukee theme, 132–33
new blood theme, 162
Noel Coward's brief encounter theme, 23–24
okay, but not at my house theme, 170–71
outdoor summer games for big kids theme, 53
pajama game theme, 145–46
pool (pocket) theme, 65–66
pool (swimming) theme, 61
progressive leaf raking theme, 125
radio days theme, 166
ragin' Cajun theme, 104
señora, que quiere? theme, 45, 47, 48–49
shangri-la-de-da (de da) theme, 95
showtime! theme, 154

212

story weaver theme, 141
strangers theme, 7
summer of love theme, 18
Sunday morning theme, 197
Venus flytrap theme, 149–51
vice-free party theme, 177
virtual party theme, 181
we're rollin'! theme, 74
whine and cheese theme, 137
wild abandon theme, 121
Forties parties
   Noel Coward's brief encounter theme, 22–26
   radio days theme, 165–68
Frank Sinatra's Real Swingin' Affair theme, 13–16

Gambling, 38–39
Games. See Entertainment

Hans Brinker, or The Silver Skates theme, 68–72
Happy Trails to You! theme, 173–75
Havana! theme, 27–30
Hide-and-Seek in the Dark and on the Floor theme, 57–59
Holidays, 86, 130
Hootenanny theme, 188–90
Hot Wax Night theme, 157–60
Houseboys, 44–49
Hubristic Tour theme, 127–30

Impressing the *objet d'amour* Venus flytrap theme, 148–52
Internet, 180, 182
Invitations
   antidote theme, 192–93
   any given Sunday theme, 77
   bakery dinner theme, 99–100
   Beethoven, books, and bull theme, 206–07
   blue plate special theme, 90–91
   Bond. James Bond. theme, 36
   Chinatown theme, 115
   come as you are theme, 183–84
   commune dinner theme, 82–83
   cookbook pass-around theme, 107–08
   divide and conquer theme, 111
   done yer duty theme, 86–87
   equinox, the solstice, and the sky theme, 202–03
   fireside chats theme, 199

Frank Sinatra's real swingin' affair theme, 13–14
fright fest theme, 2–3
Hans Brinker, or the silver skates theme, 69
happy trails to you! theme, 173
Havana! theme, 27
hide-and-seek in the dark and on the floor theme, 57–58
hootenanny theme, 188–89
hot wax night theme, 157
hubristic tour theme, 127–28
it's a marvelous night for a moondance theme, 11
magical mystery party theme, 31–32
Marrakesh express theme, 40–41
Munich meets Milwaukee theme, 131–32
new blood theme, 161–62
Noel Coward's brief encounter theme, 23
okay, but not at my house theme, 169–70
outdoor summer games for big kids theme, 52–53
pajama game theme, 144–45
pool (pocket) theme, 65
pool (swimming) theme, 61
progressive leaf raking theme, 124–25
radio days theme, 165
ragin' Cajun theme, 103
señora, que quiere? theme, 45
shangri-la-de-da (de da) theme, 94–95
showtime! theme, 153–54
story weaver theme, 140–41
strangers theme, 7
summer of love theme, 17–18
Sunday morning theme, 196
Venus flytrap theme, 148–49
vice-free party theme, 177
virtual party theme, 180–81
we're rollin'! theme, 73
whine and cheese theme, 136–37
wild abandon theme, 120–21
Island party
   shangri-la-de-da (de da) theme, 94–98
It's a Marvelous Night for a Moondance theme, 10–12

Lawn ornaments, 127–30

Magical Mystery Party theme, 31–34
Marrakesh Express theme, 40–43
Men-only party
   pool (pocket) theme, 64–67
Menu
   antidote theme, 193–94
   any given Sunday theme, 78–79
   bakery dinner theme, 100–01
   Beethoven, books, and bull theme, 207–08
   blue plate special theme, 91–92
   Bond. James Bond. theme, 36–37
   Chinatown theme, 116
   come as you are theme, 185–86
   commune dinner theme, 83–84
   cookbook pass-around theme, 108
   divide and conquer theme, 112–13
   done yer duty theme, 87–88
   equinox, the solstice, and the sky theme, 203–04
   fireside chats theme, 200
   Frank Sinatra's real swingin' affair theme, 14–15
   fright fest theme, 3–4
   Hans Brinker, or the silver skates theme, 69–70
   happy trails to you! theme, 174
   Havana! theme, 28–29
   hide-and-seek in the dark and on the floor theme, 58
   hootenanny theme, 189
   hot wax night theme, 158
   hubristic tour theme, 128–29
   it's a marvelous night for a moondance theme, 11
   magical mystery party theme, 32
   Marrakesh express theme, 41–42
   Munich meets Milwaukee theme, 132–34
   new blood theme, 162–63
   Noel Coward's brief encounter theme, 23–24
   okay, but not at my house theme, 170–71

213

outdoor summer games for big kids theme, 53
pajama game theme, 145–46
pool (pocket) theme, 65–66
pool (swimming) theme, 61–62
progressive leaf raking theme, 125–26
radio days theme, 166–67
ragin' Cajun theme, 104–05
señora, que quiere? theme, 45–46, 47, 48–49
shangri-la-de-da (de da) theme, 95–97
showtime! theme, 154
story weaver theme, 141
strangers theme, 7–8
summer of love theme, 18–19
Sunday morning theme, 197
Venus flytrap theme, 149–51
vice-free party theme, 177–78
virtual party theme, 181
we're rollin'! theme, 74–75
whine and cheese theme, 137–38
wild abandon theme, 121–22
Moondancing, 10–12
Morning parties
  blue plate special theme, 90–93
  Sunday morning theme, 196–98
Munich Meets Milwaukee theme, 131–35
Music
  antidote theme, 194
  any given Sunday theme, 79
  bakery dinner theme, 101
  Beethoven, books, and bull theme, 208
  blue plate special theme, 93
  Bond. James Bond. theme, 38
  Chinatown theme, 117
  come as you are theme, 186
  commune dinner theme, 84–85
  cookbook pass-around theme, 109
  divide and conquer theme, 114
  done yer duty theme, 88
  equinox, the solstice, and the sky theme, 204–05
  fireside chats theme, 201
  Frank Sinatra's real swingin' affair theme, 16
  fright fest theme, 4

Hans Brinker, or the silver skates theme, 71
happy trails to you! theme, 175
Havana! theme, 30
hide-and-seek in the dark and on the floor theme, 59
hootenanny theme, 190
hot wax night theme, 159–60
hubristic tour theme, 129
it's a marvelous night for a moondance theme, 12
magical mystery party theme, 33
Marrakesh express theme, 43
Munich meets Milwaukee theme, 134
new blood theme, 163
Noel Coward's brief encounter theme, 25–26
okay, but not at my house theme, 171–72
outdoor summer games for big kids theme, 53
pajama game theme, 147
pool (pocket) theme, 66
pool (swimming) theme, 62–63
progressive leaf raking theme, 126
radio days theme, 167
ragin' Cajun theme, 105–06
señora, que quiere? theme, 46, 48, 49
shangri-la-de-da (de da) theme, 97
showtime! theme, 155
story weaver theme, 142
strangers theme, 8–9
summer of love theme, 20–21
Sunday morning theme, 198
Venus flytrap theme, 152
vice-free party theme, 178–79
virtual party theme, 181
we're rollin'! theme, 75
whine and cheese theme, 138
wild abandon theme, 122

New Blood theme, 161–64
New guests, 161
Night sky, 10, 202
Noel Coward's Brief Encounter theme, 22–26

Occult, 31
Okay, but Not at My House! theme, 169–72
Oktoberfest party
  Munich meets Milwaukee theme, 131–35
Online party
  virtual party theme, 180–82
Outdoor parties
  any given Sunday theme, 77–80
  equinox, the solstice, and the sky theme, 202–05
  Hans Brinker, or the silver skates theme, 68–72
  hootenanny theme, 188–90
  hubristic tour theme, 127–30
  it's a marvelous night for a moondance theme, 10–12
  Munich meets Milwaukee theme, 131–35
  Noel Coward's brief encounter theme, 22–26
  outdoor summer games for big kids theme, 52–56
  pool (swimming) theme, 60–63
  progressive leaf raking theme, 124–26
  señora, que quiere? theme, 44–49
  shangri-la-de-da (de da) theme, 94–98
  summer of love theme, 17–21
  we're rollin'! theme, 73–76
  wild abandon theme, 120–23
Outdoor Summer Games for Big Kids theme, 52–56

Pajama Game theme, 144–47
Pajama party
  pajama game theme, 144–47
Picnics
  fright fest theme, 2–5
  it's a marvelous night for a moondance theme, 10–12
  Noel Coward's brief encounter theme, 22–26
  we're rollin! theme, 73–76
  vice-free party theme, 176–79
Pool (pocket) theme, 64–67
Pool (swimming) theme, 60–63
Potluck parties
  divide and conquer theme, 111–14
  new blood theme, 161–64

Progressive Leaf Raking theme, 124–26
Props and décor
  antidote theme, 194
  any given Sunday theme, 79
  bakery dinner theme, 101
  Beethoven, books, and bull theme, 208
  blue plate special theme, 92
  Bond. James Bond. theme, 37
  Chinatown theme, 117
  come as you are theme, 186
  commune dinner theme, 84
  cookbook pass-around theme, 109
  divide and conquer theme, 114
  done yer duty theme, 88
  equinox, the solstice, and the sky theme, 204
  fireside chats theme, 200
  Frank Sinatra's real swingin' affair theme, 15–16
  fright fest theme, 4
  Hans Brinker, or the silver skates theme, 70–71
  happy trails to you! theme, 174–75
  Havana! theme, 29
  hide-and-seek in the dark and on the floor theme, 58
  hootenanny theme, 190
  hot wax night theme, 158–59
  hubristic tour theme, 129
  it's a marvelous night for a moondance theme, 12
  magical mystery party theme, 32–33
  Marrakesh express theme, 42
  Munich meets Milwaukee theme, 134
  new blood theme, 163
  Noel Coward's brief encounter theme, 25
  okay, but not at my house theme, 171
  outdoor summer games for big kids theme, 53
  pajama game theme, 146
  pool (pocket) theme, 67
  pool (swimming) theme, 62
  progressive leaf raking theme, 126
  radio days theme, 167
  ragin' Cajun theme, 105
  señora, que quiere? theme, 46–48
  shangri-la-de-da (de da) theme, 97
  showtime! theme, 154–55
  story weaver theme, 142
  strangers theme, 8
  summer of love theme, 19–20
  Sunday morning theme, 197–98
  Venus flytrap theme, 152
  vice-free party theme, 178
  virtual party theme, 181
  we're rollin'! theme, 75
  whine and cheese theme, 138
  wild abandon theme, 122
Public transportation
  we're rollin'! theme, 73–76

Radio Days theme, 165–68
Radio shows, 168
Ragin' Cajun theme, 103–06
Remote location parties
  any given Sunday theme, 77–80
  it's a marvelous night for a moondance theme, 10–12
  okay, but not at my house! theme, 169–72
  we're rollin'! theme, 73–76
Retirement party
  happy trails to you! theme, 173–75

Sampling
  new blood theme, 162
  Señora, Que Quiere? theme, 44–49
Shangri-La-De-Da (de da) theme, 94–98
Showtime! theme, 153–56
Sinatra, Frank, 13–16, 48, 63, 152
Sixties parties
  summer of love theme, 17–21
Sock hop
  hot wax theme, 157–60
Sports
  any given Sunday theme, 77–80
  Hans Brinker, or the silver skates theme, 68–72
Stone of Shame, 176, 210
Storytelling
  story weaver theme, 140–43
Story Weaver theme, 140–43
Strangers theme, 6–9
Summer of Love theme, 17–21

Summer parties
  equinox, the solstice, and the sky theme, 202–05
  pool (swimming) theme, 60–63
  outdoor summer games for big kids theme, 52–56
  shangri-la-de-da (de da) theme, 94–98
  summer of love theme, 17–21
  Sunday morning theme, 196–98
  wild abandon theme, 120–23
Swimming party
  pool (swimming) theme, 60–63

Talent show
  showtime! theme, 153–56
Trivia games
  antidote theme, 192–95

Urban legends, 4–5

Venus Flytrap theme, 148–52
Vice-Free Party theme, 176–79
Virtual Party theme, 180–82

Waiters/waitresses, 91
We're Rollin'! theme, 73–76
Whim, parties on a
  come as you are theme, 183–88
  progressive leaf raking theme, 124–26
Whine and Cheese theme, 136–39
Wild Abandon theme, 120–23
Winetasting
  new blood theme, 163
  whine and cheese theme, 138
Winter parties
  fireside chats theme, 199–201
  Hans Brinker, or the silver skates theme, 68–72
  radio days theme, 165–68
Wisconsin, 68, 131–35, 136
Women-only party
  señora, que quiere? theme, 44–49

Also from Meadowbrook Press

✦ **The Best Baby Shower Book**
The number one baby shower planner has been updated for the new millennium. This contemporary guide for planning baby showers is full of helpful hints, recipes, decorating ideas, and activities that are fun without being juvenile.

✦ **The Best Bachelorette Party Book**
This all-inclusive book contains information on how to plan and host a great bachelorette party—plus great games, activities, and recipes. It includes the kind of spicy, fun ideas that bachelorette party-goers are looking for.

✦ **Best Party Book**
Whether it's a birthday, an anniversary, a reunion, a holiday, a retirement, a shower, or the Super Bowl, this creative guide shows even the most inexperienced host how to throw a great party.

✦ **The Best Wedding Shower Book**
This revised edition offers valuable time-tested advice on how to plan and host the perfect wedding shower with great games, activities, decorations, gift ideas, and recipes.

✦ **Games People Play**
With 180 word, drawing, memory, and trivia games for adults, adaptable to a variety of party themes, this book is funnier, faster-paced, and more entertaining and challenging than any other book of party games.

✦ **Memorable Milestone Birthdays**
Here's the only book on how to host memorable milestone birthday parties. Included are creative ideas for themes, invitations, décor, entertainment, and refreshments.

✦ **Pick-A-Party**
Party expert Patty Sachs has created the "bible" for party planners, including 160 party themes—more than any other book—to help readers turn holidays, birthdays, showers, and evenings with friends or family into special occasions.

We offer many more titles written to delight, inform, and entertain.
To order books with a credit card or browse our full
selection of titles, visit our web site at:

www.meadowbrookpress.com

or call toll-free to place an order, request a free catalog, or ask a question:

1-800-338-2232

Meadowbrook Press • 5451 Smetana Drive • Minnetonka, MN • 55343